# Praise for *Student V*

*Student voice is an often missed element of promoting a positive school climate, where students take ownership of their learning experience. This books sheds light on the importance of this topic and provides practical advice on how to let student voice take a central role in promoting learning at school.*

**—Pablo Zoido, Analyst**
Programme for International Student Assessment
Paris, France

*This book speaks to a movement that many people talk about but few act upon, Student Voice. Russell Quaglia and Michael Corso have lived their professional careers listening to students and acting on what they have heard. Now they share what it takes for education to truly become student-centered.*

**—Raymond J. McNulty, Dean of the School of Education**
Southern New Hampshire University
Chief Learning Officer
Penn Foster
Hooksett, NH

Student Voice *not only captures the urgency of our professional, societal, and moral imperatives to transform the educational system, but it also provides a thoughtful, thought-provoking, and well-researched framework for ensuring that all of our students can and will pursue and attain their aspirations. With moving stories and insights from students and teachers, heartfelt personal anecdotes, extensive analyses of data, and a deep understanding of the power of shared leadership, Dr. Quaglia and Dr. Corso have crafted a roadmap for the journey all of us as learners seek to travel—the road on which the voices of our students are the instruments of change in creating the future.* Student Voice *connects the dots of what too often seem to be disparate research about and facets of the elements of student achievement of academic, social, and personal aspirations and offers a comprehensive and coherent road to actualizing deep, meaningful, and sustainable change.*

**—Beth Havens, Educational Consultant for Innovation and Special Projects**
Horry County Schools
Conway, SC

*Schools have long told students to have goals and aspirations. But when it comes down to it, test scores and Adequate Yearly Progress stand in the paths of schools and students. This book lays out clearly that what students desire and what states require do not have to be mutually exclusive. I can't wait to share Student Voice with my colleagues.*

**—Lisa Brewster-Cook, English Teacher**
Somerville High School
Somerville, MA

Student Voice *is the result of many years of experience working with students and teachers around the world—and it shows. Drs. Quaglia and Corso have stuffed every nook and cranny of this book with practical ways to understand young people that are both sensible and profound. This is your go-to field guide for student aspirations.*

**—Adam Ray**
Pearson Foundation
Mill Valley, CA

*If you haven't considered student voice, then this book is a must read with great ideas and insightful stories that should engage you further and might just influence your practice. If you're already committed to student voice, then this book provides compelling evidence and vital structure that place student voice and aspirations front and center in education, a must-read aid to planning and implementation.*

*As we seek to increase schools' relevance in an ever more rapidly changing world, this book outlines and details a model for the way forward. Quaglia and Corso combine evidence from students, guiding principles, and conditions for their implementation in schools, stories from practice and practical notes to assist reflection and development. Written in an accessible and easy-to-read style, they together form powerful positive guidance for teaching and learning, and for change in schools.*

**—Gavin Dykes, Director**
Cellcove Ltd.
Surrey, UK

*Students routinely achieving their full potential, high performing schools becoming the new normal—*Student Voice *makes the compelling case that we "can't get there from here" without fundamentally changing the culture of schools to listen and act on what students say about their schools, their lives, and their aspirations. Refreshingly straightforward, this book provides a unique mix of profound truths and practical guidance for transforming education.*

**—Anthony Jackson, Vice President for Education**
Asia Society
New York, NY

*This book captures the essence of what has been missing in educational reform for the past several decades, in that it highlights the perspectives that matter most— the students.' Having witnessed the transformational potential of inculcating the*

*Aspirations Framework into a school, "student voice" will forever serve as the lodestar in the development of curriculum, instruction, and policy in my professional practice. The Aspirations Framework opens the door to this new era in education; in fact, student voice is the "McLuhanian" medium that will transform education in the 21st century, only if we, educators and society as a whole, take the time to listen.*

**—David E. Reilly, Assistant Superintendent**
Sequoia Union High School District
Redwood City, CA

*Quaglia and Corso champion student voice in this beautiful and inspirational narrative. This book provides a career-changing framework for educators to listen, learn, and lead; driven by the most important voice of all. My personal Aspiration is now to dream and do more to elevate student voice.* Student Voice *is a MUST READ for every educator seeking to meaningfully impact the lives of students.*

**—Dr. Lisa Kinnaman, Co-Director**
Idaho Leads Project
Boise, ID

Student Voice *is an extraordinary collection of research, success examples, common sense recommendations, and stories from the heart. I was struck by its quality, humility, simplicity, and complexity. This book is a call to action to move American public education from its fixation with test scores to winning the hearts and minds of our children "to allow our students to dream, reach, and succeed."*

**—Robert Neu, Superintendent**
Oklahoma City Public Schools
Oklahoma City, OK

Student Voice *reveals the secret to turning schools into vibrant communities of engaged learners—simply and profoundly—giving students a voice in their own learning. It offers a hopeful, poignant and elegant vision for closing the gap for the alarming number of students who are disconnected from school. Quaglia challenges educators to value student voice through intentional listening and responsive action and tells them how to create meaningful partnerships that keep students engaged, excited, and achieving. This is a must-read roadmap for reform-weary educators who will be inspired to take the less traveled path of listening to and responding to the voice of each of their students.*

**—Gail Connelly, Executive Director**
National Association of Elementary School Principals
Alexandria, VA

*In this book, Dr. Quaglia and Dr. Corso offer a successfully tested framework designed to empower students by giving them a meaningful voice in the educational process. It starts with a conversation that leads to an understanding of student perceptions of their* educational experience and ultimately creates a trusting partnership between students and educators. The partnership guides the educational process, positively influences school climate and creates an environment in which students can successfully achieve their aspirations. Student Voice *is a professional investment every school community should make.*

**—Steve York, Assistant Superintendent**
Montana Office of Public Instruction
Helena, MT

*In this magnificent book, Quaglia and Corso have unearthed a deep missing piece in learning. The elephant in the room ironically turns out to be Student Voice! And now we have it—their Aspirations, the 8 Conditions of deep learning relating to Self-worth, Engagement, and Purpose. Thanks to the authors we have a whole new set of strategies where change, learning, educators, and students merge. This is innovation at its best.*

**—Michael Fullan, Professor Emeritus**
OISE, University of Toronto

# Student Voice

*To our children . . .*

*Lauren, Casey, Chelsea, and Cali Quaglia; and Rebecca and Elise Corso*

*There are no greater teachers in the world than our children.*

*Our kids have powered us with inspiration and insight; our job was to take it somewhere!*

# Student Voice

*The Instrument of Change*

**Russell J. Quaglia**

**Michael J. Corso**

**CORWIN**
A SAGE Company

**CORWIN**
A SAGE Company

FOR INFORMATION:

Corwin
A SAGE Company
2455 Teller Road
Thousand Oaks, California 91320
(800) 233-9936
www.corwin.com

SAGE Publications Ltd.
1 Oliver's Yard
55 City Road
London EC1Y 1SP
United Kingdom

SAGE Publications India Pvt. Ltd.
B 1/I 1 Mohan Cooperative Industrial Area
Mathura Road, New Delhi 110 044
India

SAGE Publications Asia-Pacific Pte. Ltd.
3 Church Street
#10-04 Samsung Hub
Singapore 049483

Printed in the United States of America

A catalog record of this book is available from the Library of Congress.

371.8

ISBN 978-1-4833-5813-0

Executive Editor:   Arnis Burvikovs
Associate Editors:   Desirée A. Bartlett
                                    Ariel Price
Production Editor:   Amy Joy Schroller
Copy Editor:   Amy Rosenstein
Typesetter:   C&M Digitals (P) Ltd.
Proofreader:   Jen Grubba
Indexer:   Sheila Bodell
Cover Designer:   Candice Harman
Marketing Manager:   Lisa Lysne

This book is printed on acid-free paper.

SUSTAINABLE FORESTRY INITIATIVE
Certified Chain of Custody
Promoting Sustainable Forestry
www.sfiprogram.org
SFI-01268
SFI label applies to text stock

15 16 17 18 10 9 8 7 6 5 4 3 2

# Contents

# The Road Not Taken

by Robert Frost

Two roads diverged in a yellow wood,
And sorry I could not travel both
And be one traveler, long I stood
And looked down one as far as I could
To where it bent in the undergrowth;
Then took the other, as just as fair,
And having perhaps the better claim
Because it was grassy and wanted wear,
Though as for that the passing there
Had worn them really about the same,
And both that morning equally lay
In leaves no step had trodden black.
Oh, I marked the first for another day!
Yet knowing how way leads on to way
I doubted if I should ever come back.
I shall be telling this with a sigh
Somewhere ages and ages hence:
Two roads diverged in a wood, and I,
I took the one less traveled by,
And that has made all the difference.

# Preface

*I want to be good. I tried to be good. No one here [at school] understands me. Why don't they care what I am saying? Why don't they care about me? What is wrong with me?*

—Brian, high school junior

There are some things that stay with us forever. Brian was a bright, articulate student. He was a good athlete and on student council. He was the kind of student you meet and think, *Wow, the educational system is working for him.* He was one of those students who loved to get involved in things, no matter what the activity was. Students liked him, teachers enjoyed having him in class, and the principal knew him by name. From all accounts, Brian was a success story in the making.

However, as time went on his grades started to slip, his attitude was less upbeat, and he started to distance himself from his teachers. He was becoming increasingly frustrated with school. He often skipped classes and was repeatedly tardy. His grades showed it, and now he was in disciplinary trouble. He never complained, nor did he make excuses for his behavior, which made him even more endearing to me. I knew him pretty well because of the work I was doing in his school, where he was a member of the student aspirations team (a novel concept 30 years ago).

I happened to be visiting his school the day he was being suspended. Walking into the principal's office, I could see that Brian was upset. I asked him if he was okay. Obviously he was not. I asked him what had happened and he responded, "I hate this place."

"You can't hate this place," I said. "This school was made because of kids like you. You are a shining star!"

He regarded me blankly, and his eyes began to well up. Fighting back the tears (since athletes from New England don't cry), he told me, "I want to be good. I tried to be good. No one here understands me. Why don't they care what I am saying? Why don't they care about me? What is wrong with me?" Brian's raw statement would become a defining moment for me, one that in many ways set my career in motion, and inspired my dedication to understanding student aspirations and advocating for student voice. In the moment, however, and in my haste to comfort a student I cared for, I told him that everything would be fine and that I was sure things would be better when he came back.

But I never saw Brian again. After his suspension, he never returned to school. My heart hurts every time I consider that experience because I always think I could have, and should have, done more. The system failed him. I failed him. No one was listening. I was in my twenties and only wish I had known then what I know now. Maybe through some miracle he will read this book and know that I heard him— that I learned from him and am dedicated to creating better schools for all students. His voice has made a lasting difference.

This book both reflects and promotes student voice. At its heart is a fundamental conviction that students are not the problem in our schools; they are the potential. We believe student voice should be instrumental to any educational reform agenda. Our theme, therefore, is *Listen, Learn,* and *Lead.* We must not only ask young people their thoughts, but we must truly listen. We must learn from what they are saying by asking important questions and discovering *why* they feel as they do. And finally, we must utilize what we learn to be effective educators.

Student voice should never be perceived as fulfilling a mandate or thinking students have a voice because a student is placed on a few school committees. Student voice is not window dressing or some ploy to inspire students to do well on exams. We describe student voice from an operational perspective as *occurring when students are meaningfully engaged in decision making and improvement-related processes in their schools.* Student voice must become a way of being, not some plan to pay lip service to students' desire to speak out. A ninth-grade student told us, "Student voice is being able to be heard, to be listened to, then being able to change things for the better. It is one thing to be able to say what you feel, but to actually have adults listen to you and actually process what you say is totally different."

Ensuring student voice in school is not easy and must be grounded in both theory and practice. Is student voice the missing variable in our reform agenda today? We believe it is. Such new and exciting work as New Pedagogies for Deep Learning led by Michael Fullan, where student voice is integral to Dr. Fullan and his team's effort; Gavin Dykes leadership at the Education World Forum, ensuring students have a voice at the annual conference; Andreas Schleicher, Deputy Director of Education and Skills at OECD, has incorporated student voice questions in the Programme for International Student Assessment, or PISA, study; and Dawn Haywood, who leads the Student Ambassadors Board at the Aspirations Academies in England are global examples that give us hope that incorporating student voice is far more than a passing fancy, but a force to be reckoned with and a now permanent feature of the educational landscape!

Student voice is not a fad to us. Nor is it some far-off notion that will not come to fruition in our lifetime. We are seeing more examples in schools where student voice as we define it is being taken seriously and having incredible benefits for the entire educational community. We see fewer dropouts, fewer absences, engaged learners leading to greater academic success, and, most importantly, students with purpose and an understanding of who they are and want to become. For the first time, we are seeing students as active partners in their education. These student partners are not an elected or selected "special" group of students but rather cut across all ages, races, and abilities. Students with voice have one precious thing in common—they know they matter!

This book represents a new and innovative way of understanding, involving, and inspiring students. First, the *Aspirations Framework* provides a model to understand students that is based on basic constructs of dreaming and doing. Second, this model is used to identify the conditions in school that inspire students to have self-worth, be meaningfully engaged in their learning, and have a sense of purpose. Finally, we develop this *framework for action* and present concrete ways and examples that promote and encourage student voice as an instrument for change.

We take great pride being straightforward and honest; our critics call it *bold*. It is designed to share the truth of what students think about school with educators who want to make a difference. The book is driven by what happens in practice, not just theory. It incorporates data from more than one million students using the My Voice student survey and student focus groups, as well as field observations and interviews spanning three decades and several countries.

We hope this book prompts you to reflect upon your own experience and expertise, and prepares you to lead with the sure knowledge that your students can and will want to join you.

—Russell J. Quaglia

# Acknowledgments

One of the best openings of a school year we have ever witnessed was at a district in New England. The superintendent had invited three students [an eighth grader, a high school sophomore, and a senior] and their parents to the staff convocation. Each student was a kind of turnaround story. He introduced the students one at a time, briefly telling his or her tale of getting back on track. Then, after acknowledging the students' parents, he did something wonderful. He invited any administrators who had overseen buildings that these students had attended to stand. Four or five people stood. He then invited any teachers or guidance counselors who had worked with these students to stand. Another 20 people stood. For the senior about double that number rose to their feet. Finally, he asked any staff member who had interacted with the student to stand. Administrative assistants, custodians, cafeteria workers, and attendance officers all proudly stood. The applause was thunderous and the point was well made.

Anyone in the field of education knows that any one person's accomplishment is an accumulation of the efforts of many other people. No less is true of this book. You will read numerous stories from the field. Some of you may even recognize yourselves! Without the tireless work of the teachers and administrators working with students in schools every day, there would be neither a source nor a purpose for what we have written. We are privileged to have worked with so many of you in one capacity or another. In addition, there are many individuals who work in central offices and state and federal departments of education who share our concern about the current state of our educational systems and the need for involving students more in finding solutions. Your willingness to find ways to adhere to pre-existing policies while at the same time pushing the boundaries of partnership with students motivates us to keep our shoulders against the larger, slower wheel of change with you.

Between the two of us we have talked to thousands of students. Their insights and energy are our constant inspiration. Nearly all of them have known that there is a different and better way of being a community of learners. They have been excited that someone is willing to listen to their ideas and invite their participation. They are the driving force of what we do.

The Quaglia Institute for Student Aspirations (QISA) could not have a better partner or friend than the Pearson Foundation. The Foundation distributes, collects, and reports on the My Voice survey you will learn about later. They are in the vanguard of the student voice movement and, as we know too well, that is sometimes a lonely place to be! In particular, Adam Ray at the Pearson Foundation has been a faithful champion of QISA's work over the years. We are thankful for his and the Foundation's ongoing support.

All the best thinking and intentions in the world about how to make schools better for students are mere dreams without those willing to do the difficult work of implementing the Aspirations Framework in their schools. The Aspirations Academies in England and QISA's Demonstration Sites in the United States have led the way to what meaningful student involvement in decision making is all about. They have courageously overcome obstacles and the naysayers to put students first and foremost in their schools and districts. Thank you!

Finally, we are so grateful to work alongside some of the finest people and educators we have ever known and who are part of the team at QISA. Sue Harper, QISA's administrative assistant, and Deborah Young, director of operations, keep QISA running smoothly so that we can run around the world listening to students and teachers and instigating change. Megan Bedford, QISA's director of communications, was incredibly helpful in reading numerous drafts and making suggestions for layout and design. Sarah Rawlings, director of research, and her predecessor, Dr. Matthew Bundick (now at Duquesne University), have been invaluable in helping us collect, understand, and analyze the survey results that form the backbone of this book. And several members of QISA's Field Team—Dr. Brian Connelly, Dr. Kristine Fox, Julie Hellerstein, and Susan Inman—have made innumerable contributions over the years to our thinking and to this text. When you read our words, trust that their experiences, insights, and efforts are part of what you are learning.

—Russell J. Quaglia and Michael J. Corso

# Publisher's Acknowledgments

Corwin gratefully acknowledges the contributions of the following reviewers:

Sandra Burvikovs, Teacher K–5
Gifted Education
May Whitney Elementary School
Lake Zurich, IL

Peter DeWitt, Elementary Principal
Averill Park Central School
Albany, NY

Donna Eurich, Teacher
St. Clare Catholic School
North Palm Beach, FL

Lisa Graham, Program Supervisor/
Acting Director, Special Education
Berkeley Unified School District
Berkeley, CA

Jeanne Gren, Principal
Flemington Elementary School
Flemington, WV

Todd Hurst, Director of Education
and Workforce Innovation
The Center of Excellence in
Leadership of Learning (CELL)
University of Indianapolis
Indianapolis, IN

Maria Langworthy, Global Director
New Pedagogies for Deep Learning
Medina, WA

Raymond J. McNulty, Dean
School of Education
Southern New Hampshire University
Hooksett, NH

Ken Royal, Education Content Editor
Connect Learning Today; Promethean
Alpharetta, GA

# About the Authors

 **Dr. Russell J. Quaglia,** recognized globally as a pioneer in the field of education, is known for his unwavering dedication to student aspirations and student voice. Described by national news media as America's foremost authority on the development and achievement of student aspirations, Dr. Quaglia's innovative work is evidenced by an extensive library of research-based publications, prominent international speaking appearances, and a successfully growing list of ventures.

Among these ventures, Dr. Quaglia authored the My Voice suite of surveys, iKnow My Class student surveys, and the My Aspirations Action Plan, an online aspirations-based planner that helps students work toward their dreams and track their progress with the support of an adult Aspirations Advocate.

In addition to founding and leading the Quaglia Institute for Student Aspirations, Dr. Quaglia is the chief academic officer of the Student Engagement Trust, a nonprofit organization based in the United Kingdom. He also founded and currently chairs the Aspirations Academies Trust, a sponsor of primary and secondary academies in the United Kingdom built upon his aspirations research.

Combining his entrepreneurial spirit with his devotion to helping students achieve their aspirations, Dr. Quaglia established Q-Bean Coffee in 2012, a company that donates all profits from the sales of its ecofriendly coffee to educational organizations and student scholarships.

Dr. Quaglia earned his bachelor's degree at Assumption College, a master of arts degree in economics from Boston College, and master of education and doctoral degrees from Columbia University, specializing in the area of organizational theory and behavior. He has been awarded numerous honorary doctorates in humanitarian services for his dedication to students. Dr. Quaglia's work has also led him to serve on national and international committees, reflecting his passion for ensuring that students' voices are always heard, honored, and acted upon.

**Dr. Michael J. Corso** is the chief academic officer for the Quaglia Institute for Student Aspirations (QISA). He has a doctorate in education from Boston College, has been an educator for more than 25 years, and has taught at every grade level, kindergarten through graduate school. He is deeply committed to the belief that students are the agents of their own learning. This passion makes him a natural fit for work in the area of student aspirations. Dr. Corso has worked throughout his career to improve teaching and learning through teacher training and education. In his role at QISA, Dr. Corso combines research on student perceptions of their schools with educational theory and the living, breathing practice of students, teachers, and administrators.

# Introduction:
# It's Time to Listen

*Student voice is when a student expresses their opinion, it is heard by the teacher, and something is done.*

—sixth-grade male student

*I actually have a lot of ideas that could make school better for everyone—even the teachers. I don't know how to share my ideas.*

—ninth-grade female student

Every weekday morning, in every part of the world, young people embark on a journey. By bus, car, bike, or on foot, they travel from their homes, headed to what could be the best or worst, most or least important part of their day: *school*. For all the differences that could be observed across these schools, in most classrooms there would be little question as to who is the teacher and who are the learners. Age, the arrangement of desks in the classroom, how people interact, and who most often is talking, make the traditional roles perfectly clear. On the more traveled road throughout our educational history, there has always been someone older and more experienced in front of the class, firmly in the driver's seat and in charge of what is happening, and when and how it happens. Playing their part in this arrangement the learners are, ideally, a compliant group, willing to do as instructed without question, complaint, or suggestion, like children in the backseat of a car.

However, we know that this "student along for the ride" way of education is not our only option. We have been hearing about another way for some time now, though for all its endorsement in keynote presentations and research articles, it remains a road less taken: student voice. Sure, we have had student protests, student marches, student sit-ins, and student walkouts, but we are talking about student voice not that reactively opposes something, but rather *proactively participates* in the greater good of learning. We are talking about genuine and authentic student voice, where teachers ask for their students' opinions, listen—*really* listen—to what students have to say, and incorporate what they learn and students themselves into the leadership of their classrooms and schools.

The fact of the matter is that student voice is not yet a reality in most classrooms and schools. The national My Voice survey, administered to 56,877 students in Grades 6–12 in the 2012–13 school year by the Pearson Foundation, reports that just 46% feel students have a voice in decision making at their school and just 52% believe that teachers are willing to learn from students (Quaglia Institute for Student Aspirations [QISA], 2013). In that same survey, even though nearly all students (94%) believe they can be successful and two thirds (67%) see themselves as leaders, less than half (45%) say that they are a valued member of their school community. There may be thousands of students in our schools, maybe hundreds in any particular school, who, confident in their ability to succeed and ready to lead, feel shut out by adults they perceive as unprepared to listen to or value their ideas. Throughout this book we intend to listen to these students, learn from them, and lead the educational community forward in partnership with them.

All human beings want their voices to matter. We like giving our opinions and offering ideas. We want to be the subject of our activities, not the objects of someone else's. We want to be active agents, not just passive spectators. From the "terrible" 2-year-old's insistent "*I* do! *I* do!" to the adolescent's "rebellion" against adult rules, young people want to be heard and taken seriously. It's only terrible and rebellious from a certain point of view—that of the adults! From the young person's point of view, it is part of the relentless inborn drive to become a self. From his or her point of view, "My voice matters."

In the traditional school model, there is little room for student voice, so it is no surprise that less than half of students in secondary education in this country feel that they have a voice in decision making in their schools. While a clear majority of students (61%) believe they have a voice upon entering middle school, one third (37%) say they do by twelfth grade (QISA, 2013). In other words, the more our students mature, the less opportunity they have to offer their opinions and participate as leaders in meaningful ways. This finding from our work—that students experience less voice the longer they are in school—has not adequately found its way into our local, state, or national conversations and indicates we have a long way to go toward including students as partners in their education.

Students are generally self-confident and have a desire to achieve. Yet the data we present in this book show that schools typically struggle to engage, support, and make school relevant to at least half of our students. This gap could be a recipe for frustration as well as reduced performance, dropout, and ultimately a squandering of the full potential of our youth. *Or* student voice and adult listening could be the ingredients for a meaningful partnership, focused on charting a way forward together. If schools are to be places in which teaching and learning thrive, we must choose this latter, less traveled path. Listening to the voices of students can and should be the first step.

There are many ways in which student voice can have a positive impact on the educational challenges we face. When students believe their voices matter, they are more likely to be invested and engaged in their schools. When students believe teachers are listening to them, mutual trust and respect are likely to flourish. When students believe they are being heard and influencing decisions, schools become more relevant to students' lives and are more likely to be seen as serving their needs. When adults and students partner, schools become laboratories for the multigenerational, collaborative, shared decision making that is part of most contemporary businesses, organizations, and companies. In addition, students' insights, creativity, energy, and confidence offer important perspectives that can help schools improve.

As it turns out, the issue in most of our schools, both nationally and internationally, is not that we neglect to ask students questions; there are countless surveys commonly used to solicit students' thoughts on a wide range of scholastic, personal, and social issues. However, in far too many cases, these surveys are, at best, lightly regarded by adults and, at worst, dismissed as merely what the kids think. In either case, adults fail to motivate change or even initiate basic discussion with students to further understand the data. Mere asking does not qualify as listening. Listening is, in many ways, characterized by what happens next—a change in the current status quo or a clear acknowledgment that students have been heard. While it would be unrealistic to think we could, or should, accommodate every desire expressed by students, we must at the very least show that we have understood their perspective, considered it, and invite them to join us in finding solutions. Meaningful and engaging dialogue that is focused on real and important issues between teachers and their students is where student voice truly takes off.

We have listened. Our fundamental question has been: What do students think about school? Those for whom school is working generally describe it as "great"—a place to interact with friends, where teachers care, and learning happens. In its most extreme negative form, we hear students describe school as a "prison"—a metaphor for being completely voiceless. Schools as designed by adults are intended to be places where students develop both academically and socially, where they build the skills they will need to be successful beyond graduation and learn to relate and interact with others. For some students this is happening, but for far too many it is not. But how could we expect to reach 100% of students, or even most of them, *without any input from them?* Far from asking the inmates how they would run the asylum, this question—*What do students think about school?*—is critical if we are to improve our schools for all students.

# Scope, Sequence, and Student Voice

"Open your text books to chapter 1, page 1" is a traditional and common way for teachers to begin their classes. And so it goes: Chapter 2, page 14; Chapter 3, page 23; etc. Most curricula have a scope and sequence that teachers follow to unfold their curriculum. Add standards and pacing guides, and you can predict a pretty prepackaged approach to pedagogy.

One ninth-grade math teacher who engaged in Aspirations work decided to consider student voice alongside these curricular directives. Unit by unit, he asked his students to skim ahead in the chapters and share with him what they already knew or had previously covered in middle school. In one case, it led him to rearrange the chapters in a unit. In another case, he skipped a chapter completely. "We totally did this last year, like, a million times!" whined one student. An informal quiz led him to conclude that his students had indeed mastered the material in that chapter. In a third case, he learned from the students that there was a gap in their understanding that had to be filled before continuing. He drew on an eighth-grade textbook to fill that void. In addition (pun intended), as he previewed each unit with his students and checked for understanding, he discovered that most of what they knew was not connected to application. In other words, students knew about angles, but didn't know that they could use their knowledge of angles to see why some ping-pong shots work and others don't.

In every case, had he plugged along without seeking student input he would have bored some students, left others behind, and created the general impression that his teaching was more important than the students' learning. In the effort to cover material that is exactly what he would have done—covered it, obscured it, hidden it. Instead, he and his students became partners in a discovery process related to math. And for some chapters instead of reteaching the concept, he took out the ping-pong balls.

We have learned. For more than 30 years, we have been asking students and staff about their perceptions of school. We ask questions that any school could ask their own students whether in formal focus group settings or informally in classrooms, cafeterias, or corridors. Questions such as: What are your hopes and dreams? What makes you proud to be a student at our school? What does it mean for a teacher to show a student respect? Describe a lesson you found engaging and why? Share a time you felt you were a leader at school? What opportunities do you have to voice your opinions and thoughts at school? Does it matter when you speak up? Can you explain? These simple yet powerful questions are the starting point for listening to students.

Through observations, surveys, interviews, and focus groups; in assemblies, classrooms, and faculty lounges, we have invited students and staff to share what school is like from where they stand. The data we have pored over and the tales we have heard have deepened our understanding of schools and led to a profound conviction about the conditions necessary to help students and staff be successful. This book represents what we have learned from students from all over the world, and it is our hope that it will serve as a compass to inspire a new direction in education. It is time for student voice to lead us on a new journey.

## Connecting Student Voice To Aspirations

Let's say you have a choice in the morning to send your child on Bus A or Bus B. Bus A goes to a school with high academic standards and a strong, structured curriculum that is rigorous. Virtually all students are doing well academically. Yet they are doing this in an environment where teacher-student relationships are cordial at best, students are not listened to, their opinions are not sought, and creativity is an afterthought—as is students' passion for learning anything beyond what will be tested. Your student's reading skills and math skills will improve on a steady pace as they move from grade to grade.

Bus B, conversely, leaves for a school where students love to go. They can interact with each other openly, have input into what goes on every day in the classroom, and have great relationships with their teachers. The schedule is entirely flexible, conforming to the needs of the learning from week-to-week, day-to-day, and even hour-to-hour. Most assessment is formative. People come and go as they please. Driven by self-motivation, some students are doing really well, while other students are struggling. Skill level may not increase but your student will fall in love with reading and learn the everyday relevance of math.

Which bus would you put your child on?

Neither one, of course! We are looking for some combination of the two, yet when it comes to educational policy, we act as if it is an either/or proposition. Giving students a voice in their learning does not constitute chaos. And schools with high academic standards do not need to treat students like they are on a forced march to get results. There can be a third bus. One that takes students to a school where high academic achievement *is a result of* students being heard, engaged, and happy to be there. A school where reading skills improve *because* students learn to love reading. The driver of that bus is student voice.

Reading specialists, for example, know that students love to read books that interest them. This means students of all ages need to have a voice in the choice of what they read. Although *The Great Gatsby* is a classic and part of the canon of American literature, there are other well-written books that demonstrate similar themes and represent the same time period. Does every student in every tenth-grade class in a state have to be on page 20 of *The Great Gatsby* on October 30 in order to be learning effectively? Students will read and they will learn when they are given choices and options. Consider yourself as an adult learner. How engaged and involved are you when your district forces you to read a specific book, yet the book is unrelated to your job or your interests. Of course, there are times when we all must read and discuss a common text, but this should be the exception, not the rule.

Suppose we agree to put our students on Bus C, which takes them to a school where they celebrate high academic achievement *and* students are listened to, valued, engaged, and purposeful. Even this school, good as it is, is not the end of our journey. We must realize that *school is not a final destination*, but rather part of the journey that helps transport students to their futures.

## "4 Years, 4 Choices"

Recently, while visiting an urban high school in Ohio, the principal and assistant principal asked us to tag along for a new initiative they called "Principal Talking Points." Twice a month, administrators visit every classroom and convey a message. On this particular day, the message was "4 Years, 4 Choices." They shared with students that high school is a four-year process, and at the end of those four years, students could do one of four things:

1. Go to college.

2. Go to a two-year program.

3. Go into the military.

4. Begin a career (not a job, but a career).

All four choices were given equal weight and importance. The message was powerful, as administrators made it clear that it was not a choice to graduate from their high school and do nothing. We frequently heard, "Nothing is not an option" and "Our graduates do something with their lives."

Administrators talked further about what students need to do now in order to follow any one of the four paths. In addition to encouraging all students to prepare for ACTs, students thinking about the military were informed about the upcoming Armed Services Vocational Aptitude Battery (ASVAB) exam. This exam determines what career a person will pursue in the military and how the scores translate to high-level jobs. Students who wanted a career right after high school were encouraged to aim high. One administrator said, "If you want to work in a restaurant, plan to manage or maybe even own that restaurant some day."

Schooling is *a means,* not an end. That is not only true in the big picture (some have made college the goal of K–12 education, but that is like saying the goal of school is more school), but also of all the components of schooling (including assessments). Few educators would argue that the purpose of school is simply to deem students proficient on the local standardized test and graduate them. Yet our current and often myopic focus on the yearly achievement of "adequate" test scores has led us down a blind alley. The real goal (i.e., purpose/end) of school is what lies beyond the walls of K–12/16 schooling for our young people: the rest of their lives. Schools must exist for the sake of helping each and every student toward a further destination—his or her aspirations. We can only know this further destination, and so help students get there, if we are ready to listen to students' thoughts, hopes, and dreams. In this way, student voice and student aspirations go hand in hand. Thus, in *Part I: Listening,* we present the Aspirations Framework that has emerged from listening to students.

In order to truly teach our students, we must be willing to learn from them. Only they can tell us where they would like their journey to take them beyond school, and that is essential information if we are to do the important work of successfully inspiring and equipping them for what lies ahead. By inviting and encouraging their voices, and being open to what they have to say, educators create a community of collaborative learners. Far from the traditional model of teacher as the sole distributor of knowledge, in an environment of collaboration every member of the community has something to teach the group, as well as much to learn. In *Part II: Learning,* we share what we have come to understand about the principles and conditions that support students' aspirations, based on what students have told us about their experiences in school.

In *Part III: Leading,* we discuss how, given the present circumstances in education, we can move forward *in partnership with students.* Whatever the nostalgic past (open class room, back to basics, ed reform, etc.) or supposed future (21st century skills, Common Core, online learning, flipped classrooms, blended instruction, etc.) holds, we know we will not get there in our father's Oldsmobile! We need a hybrid, one that keeps the best of what has fueled effective education until now and combines it with the energy and enthusiasm of our students' hopes and dreams.

In fact, the kind of coaching that happens when we teach our children to drive a car is an excellent metaphor. The longer we work together, the more they are in control, the more they steer, the more they decide where to go. We believe all students have something to teach us, but we need to take our foot off the brake pedal and our hand off the wheel. Parents know this is no easy task. Experience, trust, and a fair bit of courage are required. But anything less and we could never hand our students the keys to their future with confidence. Letting them drive will make all the difference.

# PART I

## LISTENING

## CHAPTER 1

# Student Aspirations

*My favorite class is my CAD [computer–aided design] class. I work the hardest in that class and look forward to it every day. The 90 minutes fly by. I want to be a structural engineer in the aerospace field.*

—twelfth-grade male student

*When I grow up—I know this is crazy—but I want to own a cupcake shop. I wish we had cooking classes.*

—fourth-grade female student

"What do you want to be when you grow up?"

"Where are you going to college?"

"Have you decided on a major?"

"Have you found a job?"

"What are you doing after graduation?"

From the time we started kindergarten to the day we finished college, we recall being asked about our aspirations. Well-meaning adults and interested peers peppered us with questions about where we were headed. We offered answers ranging from vague to visionary. We mumbled, "I dunno," or answered that we aspired to be astronauts or nurses, teachers or baseball stars, inventors or veterinarians or adventurers.

As adults, similar questions arise from within:

"Is this what I want to do with the rest of my life?"

"Am I headed in the right direction?"

"Is this who I want to be?"

We all have aspirations. Aspirations may go by other names—hopes, dreams, goals—but everyone has them, from the preschooler who aspires to color within the lines to her grandmother who wants to take up painting in retirement. The human condition includes a desire to aspire. The infant's aspiration may be for food or to be held. A child may aspire to be a basketball player. The college student aspires to become a lawyer. As we mature, our aspirations take the shape of providing for and raising a family, or dedication to work, or a commitment to community outreach. For still others, aspirations involve an ultimate purpose, giving their very lives to a conviction or cause.

In school, a first grader's aspiration may be to remember to raise his hand before he speaks. That is a great aspiration at 5; however, his parents or teachers wouldn't want this to be his aspiration as a junior in high school. Similarly, a high school sophomore's most immediate aspiration might be to enter the Marine Corps after high school. Considering what to do after graduation is fairly typical for a 16-year-old, but if a 22-year-old with high school four years behind her is still wondering what she should do with her life, aspiration takes on a new sense of urgency.

## ■ ■ ■ ASSESS YOUR STARTING POINT

Use the best practices for supporting students' aspirations below to rate yourself on a scale of 0-10, where 0 is never and 10 is always.

- I know my students' hopes and dreams.

- I regularly talk with my students about their futures.

- I assess and evaluate student progress using more than just grades.

- I share my professional journey with my students.

- I provide opportunities for students to use their imaginations.

- I involve students in conferences with their parents.

- I hold high expectations for all my students.

- I make learning relevant for my students. ■

Furthermore, there are varying degrees of intensity with which each of us possesses and pursues our aspirations. Aspirations for some can be all consuming; others' aspirations are on hold while more pressing issues take precedence; and many try to balance competing aspirations. Our aspirations can vary over time in both content and power. This variation is itself part of the human experience of maturing, of becoming more and more oneself, of being engaged by the truth that learning is life-long.

In many ways, our aspirations shape the meaning and trajectory of our lives. Aspirations are what give our lives intention and direction. Our aspirations affect with whom we associate, in what activities we choose to participate, and how we spend much of our time. Understanding, reflecting on, choosing, and working toward our aspirations are large parts of who we are. However, this is only really possible if we notice that our aspirations have a present tense and not just a future one. If one has a genuine aspiration and not just a pipe dream, there is effort in the present to bring about the hoped for future. The infant aspiring to be held, presently cries; the future NBA hopeful practices free throws; and the aspiring lawyer defends the right to watch 30 more minutes of Court TV before doing homework. Aspirations are as much about what we do today as they are about where we hope to be tomorrow.

## REFLECT ON YOUR SURROUNDINGS

- Where do you see your students in the Aspirations Profile? Consider the mixture of hibernation, perspiration, imagination, and aspiration that is part of their experience in your classroom or school.

- What have you learned best moves students from hibernation, perspiration, or imagination into aspiration?

- How are you currently addressing the different profiles of the students you work with? ▪

## DREAMING AND DOING

We define aspirations as *the ability to dream and set goals for the future while being inspired in the present to reach those dreams*. Most people's common sense understanding of aspirations includes the future aspect of the definition. When answering the question "What are your aspirations?" most relate some later state: "My aspiration is to be an outstanding high school teacher." "I aspire to star in a Broadway play." "My goal is to save enough money so I can retire at 55 to fly-fish." "I aspire to be happy." Aspirations as we understand them are not simply career goals but can reference any future condition. Desiring to have a family, wanting to live a life of integrity, or hoping to make a meaningful contribution to the world are aspirations even though they are not career-specific. We should also point out that the future is an indeterminate period of time. A student may aspire to pass an important test next week, to stay out of in-school suspension this term, or to make the varsity swimming team when she goes to high school.

Aspirations are about the future, but this future-focused understanding is only half the story. The person who wants to be a high school teacher but has no clue or concern to learn how teenagers tick does not have a genuine aspiration to be a high

school teacher. We would have doubts about a person who claims to aspire to a life of integrity but who currently acts deceptively. Similarly, the aspiring Broadway star who will not audition for a school play because it makes her nervous, the aspiring test passer who does not study, and the aspiring high school swimmer who rarely practices must all be said not to have genuine aspirations.

Conversely, there are the students who take extra science courses because they know they want to be doctors and students who attend engineering summer sessions by choice because they want to get into robotics. There are students who participate in chorus, take every music elective offered, practice an instrument outside of school, and join a garage band because they see a future in the music industry. These are the students who in middle school know themselves well enough to know they love art and want to do something involving art in the future, and in the meantime they doodle, draw, and depict the world around them in the margins of their notebooks and in the sketchpads they are seldom seen without.

Aspirations are both "then" and "now." They involve both dreaming of the future and doing in the present. They are made up of a vision of where we want to get and, at a minimum, a willingness to do what is necessary to get there. When we genuinely aspire, we are facing our future *and* taking steps in the present toward it (see Ritchie, Flouri, & Buchanan, 2005; Sherwood, 1989). As teachers, if we want to support our students' aspirations as a future and present reality, we have to know them as individuals. We need to help them discover their passions, to support their pursuit of their interests, and to encourage them to dream. Sounds simple, yet how often do we actually take the time to have these conversations with our students? In some schools we have been in you would think every student had the same generic aspiration, since virtually all students are treated the same and taught in the same way.

## Try This On

In a coastal town in Maine, an elementary school holds monthly Student Interest Group sessions. Students in Grades 3-5 get to choose an interest for the year (e.g., gardening, photography, writing) and are mixed by grade level. Students in Grades K-2 have a variety of enrichment experiences they rotate through. The groups are created based on student perceptions of leadership and what it means to have a voice in their school and local community. The groups also meet a desire to have students try on a career interest.

Some of their work has included:

- A K-2 group made dog and cat toys and treats for the local animal shelter after learning about the shelter from its director.
- A Grades 3-5 group created bracelets, paper airplanes, drawings, and so on to sell during lunchtime. All proceeds went to the local soup kitchen.
- A Grades 3-5 group, with the help of the maintenance team, kept the school ground looking neat and clean. This included trash pickup, weeding the garden, breaking up ice patches in the winter, and so on.
- Another Grades 3-5 group designed and built, with the help of a group of students from the local college, a simplified version of a ropes course that they could use at recess to promote belonging, cooperation, and fun.

Through these experiences, students learned to connect their interests to a wide variety of options for their futures. While no doubt our youngest students will change who and what they will be several times as they mature, there is no question that involving them in future-thinking now both inspires them and makes school more engaging. In fact, on Student Interest Group days, the school had nearly perfect attendance!

*Source:* Susan Inman.

## THE ASPIRATIONS PROFILE

We can look at our definition graphically if we think of each aspect—present/doing and future/dreaming—as the X- and Y-axis of a grid.

**ASPIRATIONS PROFILE**

| High | Imagination<br>Sets goals for the future but does not put forth the effort to reach those goals. | Aspiration<br>Sets goals for future and puts forth effort in the present to reach those goals. |
|---|---|---|
| Future/Dreaming | Hibernation<br>Has no goals for the future and puts in no effort in the present. | Perspiration<br>Works hard in the present, but has no goals for the future. |
| Low | Present/Doing | High |

Seen this way, the two aspects of the definition provide us with four categories:

## HIBERNATION

*Having neither a future dream nor the inspiration to make any effort in the present. "What's the point?"*

Someone who does not think about the future, has no clear goals, and puts forth no effort in daily life is in the Hibernation category. Those in hibernation are stalled—they have neither a picture of where they want to go, nor the energy for doing much in the present. Such people lack a sense of purpose and rarely experience a sense of accomplishment in anything they do. In schools, we have all met the student who puts his head on the desk at the start of class, only to be poked awake by a friend. We have witnessed students idly texting under a desk. Hibernating students appear to have no interest in the present they are actually in or in what it might mean for their futures.

Think of those students who come to your classes with little to no facial expressions or excitement. Recall those students whose names you barely know. Some students in hibernation do a minimum of work so they can pass under the radar through our classes. These students can be quite easy to have as often they don't bother anyone. Educators need to ensure that during a class period every student is asked a question or somehow engaged in the learning. Some teachers choose to assign group work, while others simply walk around the room in an effort to make contact with every student. Waking a student out of hibernation does not require a profound transformation; rather, it requires the student to feel some connection and interest in learning.

## PERSPIRATION

*Working hard in the present without any connection to a future dream. "I work hard, but it's like being on a treadmill. I don't know where I'm headed."*

Perspiration is the category that describes someone who works exceptionally hard, always puts forth effort, but lacks direction or purpose. Those in perspiration rev, but don't roll. Such people are diligent, but directionless; they are often busy, but see no meaningful future in front of them. There is a thought-provoking line in the educational documentary *The Race to Nowhere* (the title and theme of which capture the category of Perspiration), in which a high school student says "Thank goodness I passed the AP French test; now I never have to speak French again!" We have met students who do everything they are asked and see the point of precious little of it. There are students who work hard in school but see no connection to the future.

Thinking back on the days when we were teaching in the classroom, we have to admit that we encouraged and enjoyed the students who were in the state of

Perspiration. They did anything we asked and always went above and beyond in all that they did. However, neither of us took the time to think or ask about their hopes and dreams. We assumed these students all had big dreams for their futures and we were confident they would reach those dreams. Now, years later, we realize our mistake. Many "perspiring" students are living out their parents' dreams and working hard because of external school or societal pressures, not because they are inwardly motivated. To help students connect their present efforts with the futures they imagine for themselves, educators must articulate why learning is taking place beyond "because it's on the test." They should encourage long-term goal setting. Teachers should congratulate effort toward goals students set for *themselves* instead of praising just "As," as grade-conscious students only perpetuate the need to work hard toward goals that are not necessarily their own and do not extend beyond the report card.

## COMMIT TO A DIRECTION

- Ask students regularly about their hopes and dreams.

- Incorporate student interests in teaching. Even casual references to a hobby will engage students.

- Don't allow students to sleepwalk through classes. Involve these students in making classes more engaging.

- Ride the school bus at least twice a year to understand students' preschool journeys.

- Greet students when they enter the classroom. ■

## IMAGINATION

Dreaming about the future, but being uninspired to work in the present toward that dream. "My future will be handed to me, there's no need to work for it."

Those who can readily share their future plans but show little, if any, effort to reach those dreams comprise the category of Imagination. Here we hear about beautiful and exotic destinations but see little evidence of the engine required to bring the future to reality. Such people have positive attitudes about their prospects, but they take no steps in the present to reach their goals. Some of our favorite students are in this category. They tell us about plans to go to Ivy League colleges (when they are barely passing our classes), to open their own businesses (when they never have had jobs), or to start for the local professional teams (when they don't play on the school teams). These students dream big—and we like that—but they don't *act* in a big way.

A friend who teaches sixth grade recently shared that he has his most creative and lively class in recent memory. Since this friend has a hard time sitting for more than five minutes, he loves the energy of this group of students. He admitted, however, that many of his students also talked big in regards to their current lives and futures. To help his dreamers become a bit more grounded, he changed his approach. At the beginning of every week, students were required to develop an academic and a social/personal goal for the week. Of course, this was initially met with many groans. However, he was determined to help his students live the connection between dreaming and doing. Students had to develop new goals each week, and the goals had to be shared with the teacher and at least one peer. On Fridays, the entire class discussed goal attainment.

After a few months, his relentless efforts with goal setting began to pay off. Students no longer needed guidance on what an acceptable and realistic goal looked like, and they were able to articulate the connection between goals (dreams) and effort (doing). The teacher then started having students develop monthly goals instead of weekly goals. Although this process went through the same initial challenges as weekly goal setting, by the end of the year, he felt all his students were skilled and competent at setting and achieving weekly and monthly goals. Working with students in Imagination means teaching students how to reach their short- and medium-term goals and develop opportunities for even the nearest dreams to become reality.

## OVERCOME OBSTACLES

**Our student population is too transient to build relationships.** A transient population is a real issue in many schools, but you build relationships with students one at a time. Knowing just *one* thing about each of your students can make a difference.

**Some students are disengaged no matter how hard we try.** We don't need to try harder, we need to try *differently*. Students are generally not engaged because they see no relevance or value to what they are learning. Learn a student's hopes and dreams and integrate that into a lesson. The results will not only be a more engaged student, but one who will gain a whole new respect for you.

**The state requires our school to evaluate students on math, science, and English, not student aspirations.** We must first accept the fact that having aspirations is not separate from doing well in school. We have learned that when students connect what they are learning to their futures, they are 15 times more likely to be academically motivated (QISA, 2013). Aspirations is not another mandate. It is a framework for doing everything schools already do, but in a meaningful and relevant manner.

**Dealing with student aspirations is the counselor's job, not mine.** This common misperception is that aspirations work belongs outside the classroom. However, developing a teaching and learning environment that supports students as individuals, engaged learners, and potential leaders requires changes in classroom practice. ∎

## ASPIRATION

*Having a dream for the future and being inspired in the present to work toward that dream. "I create the future I want through my present efforts."*

Those with Aspirations are determined. With genuine aspiration comes the vision of a destination clearly seen and the passion for exerting oneself on behalf of that future. Such people have the ability to set goals for themselves while being inspired in the present to work toward those goals. Those with aspirations have a clear intention about what they want to do and who they want to become: They commit the energy, time, and resources required to meet their objectives. The high school junior who seriously tells you she wants to be President and, because she founded and currently runs the school's civics club, you believe she can make it happen or the student who wants to build world-class yachts and who apprentices with a local carpenter every summer and on weekends, or the student who has maxed out the assignments in his computer-aided design class because he dreams of being a structural aerospace engineer all have aspirations.

Over our careers, we have been fortunate to work with and meet many students who epitomize aspirations. Recently, in an effort to develop a student advisory board, we asked students to share their thoughts on success. A sophomore wrote the following: "What motivates me to be successful is my future and the future of others. Success to some people is determined by how much money you have or all the nice things you have. Yes those are nice perks, but to me being successful is having a roof over my head, a loving family and waking up every day knowing I am making or trying to make a difference. How successful you are is determined by how hard you are willing to work to reach your goal. For some people these things may be harder and you may have more challenges to face, but nothing is impossible. I know if I want a great future, I have to do everything in my control to make it happen. In my eyes success means so many different things."

# ARRIVE

In schools that foster students' aspirations:

- Students talk about their futures beyond high school.
- Students know learning is about more than test scores.
- Teachers know students' hopes and dreams.
- Teachers make learning relevant for students.

- Administration organizes career, college, and postsecondary fairs for students to explore their options.
- Administration strives to offer myriad courses to engage all learners in the building.
- Community members share their professional journeys with students. ∎

The quadrants of the Aspirations Profile betray an obvious fact: Our aspirations operate on a dynamic continuum, more so than in a static set of boxes. We may be in hibernation as we mindlessly recover in front of a television show after a long day at school, but that is not our permanent state. We may be in perspiration temporarily because our supervisor has given us an important task without a clear picture of how it fits in with the larger project. Shoveling snow after a winter storm, our imagination may consider how nice it would be to move south, knowing full well we have no plans to do this. We are not all aspiring all the time. Yet when we are aspiring, the full meaning of who we are comes into focus. We are most ourselves, not when we are dozing or driving ourselves out of sheer duty or daydreaming. We are most ourselves when we are taking action to bring about the goals we have set for ourselves. We are most ourselves when we are in the very process of becoming who, not just what, we want to be.

CHAPTER 2

# The Aspirations Framework

*Teachers who care don't try to form you as a person, or force you in a direction; they guide you and respect you as you are. They find out your history and struggles to find out how they can help you. It's specific to who you are, and not just a template of what they force on everyone.*

—tenth-grade male student

*Schools should take a day to see what students are feeling about school, classes, and teachers. They should ask and check-in with students periodically to see if students are understanding what school is about.*

—eighth-grade female student

It is one thing to be able to accurately define Aspirations as something more than pipe dreams. It is another thing to say schools should be places that are not only about test scores, but also about helping young people move out of hibernation, imagination, or perspiration so that they can achieve their dreams. It is yet a third thing—and we might add the most important thing—to move beyond these lofty ideals and commitments to actually implementing in schools the conditions that inspire students to reach their fullest potential. And so the definition of aspirations and the Aspirations Profile outlined in the previous chapter are the first part of a framework that schools can use to help students become successful academically, personally, and socially.

Use the best practices for supporting student voice below to rate yourself on a scale of 0-10, where 0 is never and 10 is always.

- I regularly ask students for classroom feedback.
- I co-teach with students.
- I learn from my students.
- I use student input to improve my teaching.
- I invite students to department, committee, and grade-level meetings.
- Students are educational partners in my classes.
- Students help develop classroom rules.
- Students are responsible for assessing parts of their schoolwork. ■

In the Aspirations Framework, movement out of hibernation, perspiration, and imagination toward aspirations is guided by three principles that show up again and again, not only in the research, but also in the core beliefs, values, and mission and vision statements of educators and schools that support student aspirations. In turn, these 3 Guiding Principles that form the second part of the Framework, and characterize an environment that fosters student aspirations, are operationalized through 8 Conditions, the third part of the Framework. Completing the Framework is a comprehensive student survey that measures the Principles within a school environment so that educators can identify which Conditions to improve in support of student aspirations.

The Aspirations Framework has been two decades in the making. Nearly 20 years ago, through a combination of field research and meta-analysis undertaken to identify previous research on the many variables that influence student achievement and success (Quaglia & Cobb, 1996), the grounded theory known as Student Aspirations was developed. Current research continues to support this theory, and although there are endless variables in schools that influence student growth and development, a road map for fostering aspirations consistently emerges in successful schools—and is consistently missing in struggling schools.

We want to be clear: The Aspirations Framework is not a program. There is no implementation binder. There is no single way to live out the 3 Guiding Principles or the 8 Conditions. As a framework, Aspirations is an organizing conceptual map for movement. The Aspirations Framework provides a destination: Every student has the ability to dream about the future and be inspired in the present to get there. The Framework indicates the major highways to achieve this goal: Ensure the Self-Worth, Engagement, and Sense of Purpose of every student. The Framework provides the on-ramps for those highways: Belonging, Heroes, and Sense of Accomplishment lead to Self-Worth; Fun & Excitement, Curiosity & Creativity, and Spirit of Adventure lead to Engagement; and Leadership & Responsibility and Confidence To Take Action lead to Purpose. However, because Aspirations is not a program, there is no information about what vehicle you should use, what to have for lunch on the journey, or where and when to stop for gas. How a school improves any of the conditions depends entirely on the state of those conditions and what those in the school choose to do to improve. We do have some strong opinions about who the drivers should be!

When a school adopts the Aspirations Framework, there will undoubtedly be programmatic elements—a new advisory program (to implement Heroes), a shift to blended or project-based learning (to implement Engagement), a student-led opening of the school year (to implement Leadership & Responsibility)—but these are for the school to decide in partnership with their students. It would be awfully presumptuous of two guys writing a book in Maine to make pronouncements about what should happen in every classroom and in every school around the country. We feel perfectly comfortable saying that educators should provide every student with every opportunity to put forth every effort into achieving their dreams.

As a conceptual map, unlike many programs, the Aspirations Framework is applicable at any level of educational experience. A classroom teacher can work to ensure the Self-Worth, Engagement, and Purpose of her students even as the rest of the building goes on with business as usual. A school or district can decide to use the Framework as a way of organizing the myriad programs it has implemented over the years, lending coherence to an otherwise incoherent accumulation of "flavor of the month" initiatives. We have seen entire communities work together to promote experiences for young people that align with the Guiding Principles and Conditions of Aspirations work.

## GUIDING PRINCIPLES

The 3 Guiding Principles that support students' aspirations are as follows:

- **Self-Worth**
  Self-Worth occurs when students know they are uniquely valued members of the school community; have a person in their lives they can trust and

learn from; and believe they have the ability to achieve—academically, personally, and socially.

- **Engagement**
  Engagement happens when students are deeply involved in the learning process as characterized by enthusiasm, a desire to learn new things, and a willingness to take positive, healthy steps toward the future. Students are meaningfully engaged when they are emotionally, intellectually, and behaviorally invested in learning.

- **Purpose**
  Purpose exists when students take responsibility for who and what they are becoming. This involves not only choosing a career, but also deciding to be involved, responsible members of their community. Purpose is as much about who students want to be as it is what they want to do.

## REFLECT ON YOUR SURROUNDINGS

- How do you gather feedback from your students about their view of their learning environment?

- What compelling or consistent message do you hear from students

about the conditions that affect their learning?

- When students offer their opinions and ideas, how does it change what you do as an educator? ∎

## CONDITIONS IN SCHOOL

These Guiding Principles are operationalized in school environments in quite specific ways. We refer to these as the *8 Conditions That Make a Difference*. Schools create Self-Worth when educators, as well as systems and structures, support the Conditions of:

**Belonging:** The belief that a student is a valued member of a community, while still allowing him or her to maintain his or her uniqueness.

**Heroes:** The everyday people in students' lives who inspire them to excel and to make positive changes in attitudes and lifestyles.

**Sense of Accomplishment:** The recognition of effort, perseverance, and citizenship—along with academic achievement—as signs of student success.

# Child's Eye View

Never underestimate the power of student voice and the importance of what students have to share.

Several years ago we were conducting focus groups with kindergartners. Yes, they were squirmy and all over the place, and my respect for kindergarten teachers doubled after a full day of sessions. During one of the groups a young boy, Marcus, said, "School would better if I wasn't always thirsty." Where I promptly replied, "Oh you should drink more." Marcus kept insisting that he was *soooo* thirsty all the time. I started to wonder if he had a health issue or something his teacher knew about that made him so thirsty.

Marcus was adamant that I was going to listen to and understand him. He stood up, took my hand and said, "Let me show you." I was hesitant—what was he going to show me? Where was he taking me? So I followed Marcus down the kindergarten hallway. He pointed at the water fountain. "See, see, see!" I did not "see." Marcus chimed in, "I can't reach the water fountain." How simple it was to become Marcus's hero once I saw from his point of view. Together we found the custodian, and he found the stools that the adults had forgotten to put out at the beginning of the school year. Yes, listening to student voice can make the difference between a bad and good school day, week, month, or year.

*—RJQ*

Schools create Engagement when educators, as well as systems and structures, support the Conditions of:

Fun & Excitement: Students being actively engaged and emotionally involved in their schoolwork.

Curiosity & Creativity: Inquisitiveness, eagerness, a strong desire to learn and develop new or interesting things, and a longing to satisfy the mind with new discoveries.

Spirit of Adventure: Students' ability to take on positive, healthy challenges at school and at home, with family and with friends.

Finally, schools create a sense of Purpose when educators, as well as systems and structures, support the Conditions of:

Leadership & Responsibility: Students being able to express their ideas, make decisions, and show a willingness to be accountable for their actions.

Confidence to Take Action: The extent to which students believe in themselves and act on behalf of their goals when others have high expectations of them and provide support when needed.

## COMMIT TO A DIRECTION

- Ask students what they thought of a specific lesson: Too hard? Too easy? Relevant?

- Provide time for your students to ask questions during class.

- Create opportunities for students to post questions and thoughts about class that come directly to you.

- Invite students to review classroom and school policies and procedures.

- Conduct student focus groups at least once a quarter. ▪

How a particular school fosters each Condition may be unique. The Framework itself only indicates that Belonging is important for developing Self-Worth, in the effort to nurture students' aspirations. It does not propose *how* any school should develop Belonging. What would improve Belonging in Birmingham might not work in the Bronx. The cliques in a high school vary from school to school, as does the permeability of their boundaries. Some schools have an advisory program that supports the Condition of Heroes, others do not. One school may have an interdisciplinary, project-based curriculum that fully engages students in their learning, whereas another school may offer students rote information in the silos of the academic disciplines. In order to learn how to build upon the Framework in ways that are unique to their school, educators need to know where they stand with respect to the Framework in the eyes of *their* students.

## OVERCOME OBSTACLES

**Listening to students takes time.** Yes, it does. As we know, there is little wiggle room to administer surveys, ask students their opinions on various matters, and then consider what they have to say. Yet at the same time, there is nothing more important we could be doing. Time sacrificed in the short run to listen to students pays off in the long run in the form of higher engagement, fewer student management issues, and greater student investment in the learning environment. One thing we have learned is that we must be purposeful in carving out time to listen to student voices. Sadly, it does not happen naturally . . . yet!

**Some staff members believe students don't have anything worthwhile to share.** Recently, while conducting a professional development session, several teachers stated, "I am the expert and I really doubt students can add anything useful that will make a difference." First, we must realize the simple fact students do have something to teach us. They have points of view that are uniquely their own and can provide insights into their world that we will never know about until we learn to ask and listen. ■

## LEARNING TO LISTEN

In the early days of implementing the Aspirations Framework in the field, with all grade levels and in diverse settings, a long and arduous process to develop an instrument that would measure this model was undertaken. Steps included pilot surveys, field tests, student and staff interviews and focus groups, and reliability analyses. Great care was employed not to violate the privacy of students in order to get the most truthful responses, while at the same time ensuring the data being gathered would be useful for schools. After several years of testing, data gathering, and analysis, along with further fine-tuning over the years, we now have an instrument with 69 items to measure the 3 Guiding Principles that affect the growth and development of students and their aspirations—the My Voice Student Survey.

My Voice asks students to respond to statements about their school environment as well as six demographic questions. Students respond to the statements on a five-point Likert scale ranging from "Strongly Agree" to "Strongly Disagree." The survey takes approximately 15 minutes to complete. Whenever a school takes My Voice, every student completes the instrument; as a result, there is no sampling error in the report. This provides each school with a solid foundation for interpretation and closes the door on wondering whether those who responded happen to be "ax-grinders" or, conversely, those who see the school "through rose-tinted glasses." In addition to avoiding sampling error, this every-student approach mitigates the responses of students who do not take such surveys seriously. In any given school there are undoubtedly a few such students. When every student is surveyed, those who answer willy-nilly simply cannot have a meaningful impact on the final numbers. We are confident that the aggregate results presented in this book reflect the general sentiments of the entire student body at the schools that were surveyed. Given the number and diversity of schools surveyed, they are also an accurate reflection of what students across the country think about school.

The current version of the My Voice Student Survey (for students in Grades 6–12) has been administered nationwide for seven years. In all, close to one million students have been surveyed. When one compares the results from year to year, they are remarkably consistent. At least as far as students are concerned, not much has changed in schools. The following data representing the voice of students are from the most recent My Voice survey at the time of publication. During the 2012–13 academic year, the My Voice Student Survey was completed by 56,877 students in Grades 6–12. Schools taking the survey did so of their own initiative and worked with the Pearson Foundation to administer the survey to all students. The 200 schools represented various sizes and socioeconomic backgrounds, from nine states across the United States (Arkansas, California, Indiana, Louisiana, Massachusetts, Maine, Montana, Ohio, and Texas). The gender and grade-level breakdowns were roughly evenly distributed, and the sample was both racially and socioeconomically diverse (see Appendix A).

By asking students how they perceive their school environment, My Voice provides us with a powerful tool for understanding both what motivates and inspires students to achieve and how well students believe schools are meeting those objectives. Far too often, students cannot reach their future goals and dreams because the conditions around them do not support their desire to do so. As a result, their motivation flags, aspirations falter, and achievement falls. Assessing the current state of the teaching and learning climate in schools is an essential first step toward positive change. Toward this goal, My Voice helps us uncover what students think, believe, and feel about their schools.

Taken together, Aspirations (a goal of schooling), the 3 Guiding Principles (research grounded beliefs about what enables students to aspire), the 8 Conditions (the way educators and schools live out the Guiding Principles), and the My Voice results (a tool for assessing the Guiding Principles in a school from the students' point of view) provide educators with a practical framework for achieving academic, as well as personal and prosocial outcomes. This framework can be used to guide the development of educational experiences, from the individual classroom to the entire school building, from casual teacher-student conversations in the cafeteria to decisions about scheduling. If school curriculum, activities, lessons, co-curricular experiences, behavior management policies, and so on all work to set in place the 8 Conditions, students will develop self-worth, be engaged in their

# 18

Not sure if my daughters or their friends appreciated this, but I was always doing research: Asking questions about school, teachers, sports, clubs. One day I was driving a carful of seniors to school and I asked, "Do you think students have a voice at your school?" They all chuckled as if it were a ridiculous question.

One girl (later the valedictorian of her class) answered, "Mr. Corso, I'm 18 years old. I can vote. I can serve on a jury. I can open my own checking account. I could get married without my parents permission. I can buy a house if I had the money. And I am allowed to join the army and go to another country and kill people. But between 8 a.m. and 3 p.m., I have to ask a teacher's permission if I want to pee."

There may be all kinds of reasons why we restrict students' movement in school. Why we start from a stance of distrust rather than trust. Why we have hall monitors and hall passes and late slips. But make no mistake about how even the "good" kids view this. It is not just restrictive in their eyes; it seems stupid.

What would schools look like if they started from a position of trusting kids? What would school rules look like if the fundamental stance of the system was that most of the time, most of the students do the right thing? What if, inevitably, when a student made a poor choice, we held *that* student accountable, rather than tried to prevent the inevitable with blanket rules that made every student feel like a suspect?

*—MJC*

classes and the life of the school, and have a sense of purpose. Furthermore, students with high aspirations show marked improvements in academic achievement and social awareness (Deci & Ryan, 1985; Eccles & Wigfield, 2002), and they make positive contributions to their school community. When all students believe in themselves, are engaged in their learning, and understand that what they learn today influences who they are becoming, then the larger goal of helping students reach their fullest potential will finally be met.

## ARRIVE

In schools that promote student voice:

- Students are eager to share their thoughts and opinions because they know they matter.

- Students are not afraid to ask questions in class.

- Teachers believe students are partners in the education process.

- Teachers seek student input and guidance on a regular basis.

- Administrators involve students in building-wide decisions and committees.

- Administrators value student feedback for teacher evaluation.

- Community members expect students to have a voice and seat with the school board.

- Community members regularly conduct focus groups with students. ■

# PART II

---

## Learning

## CHAPTER 3

# Reality Is Not the Enemy

*We don't want school to be a boring place.*

—eighth-grade male student

*I work hard for teachers who show me they care. And I sometimes don't do my work when I know a teacher doesn't care.*

—eleventh-grade male student

Not everyone likes every mirror they look in. Some widen, others slim. Some shorten, others elongate. Assuming, however, one is not in a funhouse (not always a safe assumption), there is a more or less accurate picture of reality one must regard in the looking glass. Schools see themselves in a variety of mirrors. There is no want for educational instruments that reflect back to a school its condition from various angles—from standardized tests to drug and alcohol surveys, from math metrics to leveled reading exams. From these myriad yardsticks spring a labyrinth of branching interpretations. Add longitudinal, trend, gender, socioeconomic, and scale analyses, and it is no wonder most educators' eyes glaze in the soft white glow of the LCD projecting data.

My Voice results may seem like just one more set of sleep-inducing statistics. However, as we have worked with schools and their results, we have seen an opposite effect. My Voice data—representing the voice of students—serve as a wake-up call, rather than a lullaby. Like driving a car on auto-pilot and hearing a honk that the light has turned green, teachers and administrators respond with renewed attention and focus to the road they are on and the destination they have set for themselves. The truth is that every time these data are presented, there are not many surprised people in the audience—whether adults or students. As a matter of fact, we frequently hear comments like, "I thought student boredom would be worse," or "I had a sense that our students really don't know how much we care," or a favorite from parents, "I bet that is what the data would have said when I was in school."

While we have done (some might say overdone) a good job asking students *what they know* in school, we need to do a much better job asking students *what they think, believe, and feel* about school. As we have mentioned, our passion for education takes us all over the world. We cannot get off a plane, check out of a hotel, or return a rental car without our mobile devices asking us to respond to a survey asking, "How did we do?" To be sure, we are not fans of the "students as customers" approach to school, but we are advocates for a "students as partners" approach. It is difficult to argue that the students' point of view is irrelevant to any effort to improve what we do as educators.

## ■ ■ ■ ASSESS YOUR STARTING POINT

Use the best practices for using student voice data below to rate yourself on a scale of 0-10, where 0 is never and 10 is always.

- I value student perceptions of their school experiences.
- I use student perspectives to inform my teaching.
- I regularly check in with students to learn about their lives.

- I stay current with pop culture and events that shape the lives of my students.
- I believe that I have something to learn from my students.
- I include student voice data in my professional goals.
- My students trust me.
- I make myself available to listen to students. ■

## LISTENING TO LEARN

There are three important concepts we ask schools to keep in mind when analyzing the data from My Voice. These should also be kept in mind as we look at the aggregate in this book:

1. The results reflect respondents' perceptions of reality.

2. The data are merely numbers.

3. The most helpful comparisons are internal.

## PERCEPTION IS DIFFERENT FROM REALITY, BUT PERCEPTION SHAPES REALITY

My Voice is an opinion survey. As such, the results reflect students' perceptions of reality, not reality. That is not to dismiss the results (as some are inclined to do) as *merely* students' perceptions or opinions. We have heard teachers say, "That's just what the students think; we know what the truth is." On the contrary, students' perceptions shape what they think and how they act in a school, and so provide an accurate picture of a school's climate and culture. That is true for *everyone*. No one actually deals in reality; everyone operates only out of his or her perceptions of reality. Reality is complex; to truly understand it, we need various points of view.

As educators we ask students for their opinions all the time. The questions we ask range from "What do you think will happen at the football game tonight?" to "What are your thoughts on the recent election?" Many teachers also ask students for feedback on classes, exams, and specific units. These efforts at engaging students through their opinions are all part of good teaching. What is different about the approach we are recommending is that we believe schools need to develop systematic and intentional ways to gather student opinions. This allows the collected data to be tabulated, analyzed, and used alongside other types of data collected in schools. When students' perceptions are gathered in this way and put in dialogue with the staff's perceptions, insights emerge and can form a basis for sound decision making and action.

Remember that children's story about the five blind men examining an elephant with their hands? The one at the front touching the trunk says, "It's a snake." From the tail someone responds, "No. It's not big enough to be a snake. It's a worm." The man alongside says, "It's a barn." With his arms around a leg, the fourth man says, "It's a tree." Finally, feeling the ear, the fifth man concludes, "It's a fan." Their perceptions are all accurate but limited. It's not until they share their various viewpoints that they conclude that each had only one piece of reality and that what they are examining is an elephant. If we continue to make decisions and act as if students' opinions are unimportant or unnecessary and if we continue to exclude student voice from our school improvement plans, building leadership teams, department meetings, and various other committees, then we are operating in the dark as well.

## DATA ARE MERELY NUMBERS

One of the reasons we don't understand the term *data-driven decision making* is that data are merely numbers. Data are inanimate. They have neither intelligence nor will. How can they drive decisions? Professional educators, *informed by data*, should drive decisions in a classroom, school, or district. That is a characteristic of being a professional: decisions are informed by data, not just by anecdotes or personal experiences. The number 40% means nothing in and of itself. What decision would it drive absent a context, an interpreter, and a judgment about its accuracy and value?

Suppose we told you that we had a person who used to work with us who had a failure rate of 60%. That's right: 6 out of every 10 times this person did a particular part of his job, it was a disaster. He was unproductive, did not advance our cause at all, and, three fifths of the time, he was absolutely no help. As those who supervised him, what would you counsel us to do with him? Would you recommend we provide him more training, suggest he try another line of work, flat out fire him, or pay him millions of dollars so he never leaves our organization?

The final option might seem a bit odd except for the fact that we have withheld a vital piece of information: He is a baseball player, and the particular job he failed at *only* 6 out of every 10 times was getting up to bat. With a batting average of .400 he would surpass the greatest players in the game. If we were baseball general managers instead of educators, we would be paying this employee millions of dollars.

How rich is the context within which you interpret data? Do you have all the information you need to develop valid understandings? Are your standardized reading scores set alongside survey, focus group, and observation data that reveal whether students enjoy reading? Are your math scores judged in light of data that measure whether students are learning how to apply math to their everyday lives? Do your science assessments indicate that students are learning how to think scientifically as well as memorize relevant scientific facts? Many schools put their test scores in the limited context of socioeconomic status, but we are arguing for a context that includes everything about students—their hopes, dreams, interests, and potential.

When interpreting student survey results, the same rule of thumb applies. Data are merely numbers. Numbers contain no insights, judgments of fact or value, decisions, or action plans. Mistakes some make when reading a student survey are

1. Moving too quickly from data to judgment of fact:

"We correctly understand what students are saying."

Adult interpretation of terms like "pride," "respect," and "interesting" can differ from a young person's understanding of those same terms. We highly recommend checking adult interpretations with students in focus groups. Think of how many times in interactions with other people, the source of misunderstanding is a different interpretation of the same reality.

We learned this early on when discussing the issue of school pride with some middle school students. One of the statements on My Voice associated with Belonging is "I am proud of my school." Adults have a tendency to interpret pride in school in terms of school spirit and morale—intangible qualities that are important to feeling connected and a part of something bigger than oneself. As we interviewed a group of seventh graders about their low school pride results, we had in mind a remedy that included new coaches and pep rallies and banners.

When we asked students why they thought so many of their peers were not proud of their school, they started to tell us about peeling paint on their lockers and a gym roof that had been leaking for two years. They interpreted the word *school* in terms of physical plant—something quite tangible and concrete. Had we not talked to the students, had we let My Voice data drive the decision, our adult lens would have had us firing coaches and pulling students out of class for rah-rah assemblies. Instead, we brought families in for a fun day of painting lockers and held a fund-raiser for repairing the roof.

**2. Jumping from data to judgment of value:**

"This is bad." Or "This is good."

We are convinced that so many initiatives fail to take root in schools, not because they are based on bad data or research, or a lack of accurate understanding. They fail because the people asked to implement the initiative do not actually care.

Let us be clear, administrators and teachers working in schools care about students. They care about their academic success; they care about their personal, social, and emotional well-being; most care about the subjects they teach. What they do not care for is the passing parade of programs purported to help them and their students. That's why so much effort is expended by leaders on "buy in" or "enrollment." Without it, any change effort is doomed to failure. Yet in our experience, efforts to establish the value of a new program to those asked to implement it fall short. Thus, the initiative fails and a new initiative is brought in only to fail and a new initiative is brought in . . . and on it goes.

One advantage of the Aspirations Framework is that for most educators, it represents the reasons they went into education in the first place. While we have run across the occasional AP calculus teacher who cannot see how Fun & Excitement is part of her job, for the most part, teachers take to the 8 Conditions. They not only see the value of Belonging to academic achievement, they already work to establish a classroom where students feel connected. Most teachers wish they could create more Curiosity & Creativity in their classrooms. We have yet to meet the building principal who wants less Leadership & Responsibility in his student body.

Having said that, not all student survey results are relevant to a particular school. A school's agreed-upon objectives, values, mission, and vision should be a part of the conversation. Student voice is neither a slap in the face nor a pat on the back. Once a school knows that it understands the students correctly from focus groups, it must consider whether the results matter to its overall objectives as a learning community.

### 3. Leaping from data to action planning:

"We have to *do* something about this."

Far too often, we have seen data blindly lead to rash decisions. If writing scores are low, schools implement writing across the curriculum. And so a physical education teacher with little training in assessing essays is asked to assign writing. A math teacher must take time away from teaching math skills so students can journal about math. Schools shorten recess to have more instructional time because of data, without regard for what impact a lack of movement has on the growing bodies of those they instruct. We are not opposed to writing across the curriculum or students spending time on instruction. We are questioning an "If this data, then that action" approach, which short circuits input from the teachers and students on whom the action will have the biggest impact.

Student opinion surveys are not immune from this truncated approach. But to leap from a high "I think bullying is a problem in my school" result on any survey to a zero tolerance policy for bullying would be as misguided as cancelling recess to do more reading. At the risk of overstating it: *We have to talk with the students.* We have had a conversation like this more than once with a group of students:

> Interviewer: So 64% of students at your school agreed that bullying is a problem in your school. What do you think?
>
> Students: Yes. It is definitely a problem.
>
> Interviewer: Have you ever been bullied?
>
> Students: No.
>
> Interviewer: Have you ever bullied someone? Be honest!
>
> Students: No.
>
> Interviewer: Have you ever seen bullying?
>
> Students: Not really. Fighting, maybe. But not bullying.
>
> Interviewer: Then why do you think bullying is a problem?
>
> Students: Well, we have had three antibullying assemblies and the teachers all have these no bullying posters in their rooms and at least once a week our principal makes an announcement about not bullying, so it must be a problem!

Our approach is to have professional educators—those who work with the students every day—as well as the students they work with every day (the foremost experts being students in that building) drive decisions based on the information they receive from surveys and focus groups.

- How do data from your students inform your decision-making process? Is such data limited to summative assessments?

- What positive changes have you seen as a result of learning from your students?

- When making decisions, how do you consider multiple points of view—your own and those of students, parents, observers, and so on?

- What are some of the questions you would like to ask your students to better understand their experience of school?

- What have you learned about the way the teaching and learning environment supports academic achievement?

- How would you change a school culture that is resistant to student voice so that student voice can be heard? ■

Interpreting the results is a process of moving from data to insights (What do these numbers mean?), to judgments of fact (Have we understood the data correctly?), then to judgments of value (Is this important to us?), and finally, to action (What should we do?). This process begins with inquiry and dialogue among colleagues. In these conversations, school staff can question the data and form hypotheses that might explain the results. For example, if only 35% of students report feeling proud of their school, what might be the source of that diminished pride? A lack of success in sports? An aging school building? Failing to meet adequate yearly progress?

While the process begins with collegial conversation, it must not end there. "Analysis paralysis" among the adults is a real danger and can be avoided by inviting students to the conversation. Focus groups with students help adults learn whether they have correctly understood what students are saying. Only when staff verify that they correctly have understood the data can they decide what actions to take to improve the Conditions that affect students' aspirations. And students must be part of the effort to improve the Conditions. Student voice, adults who listen, and then a partnership of action create the path that leads to a better school.

## COMPARE INWARDLY

Many schools want to interpret their results in comparison to a national or state aggregate. In subsequent chapters, we will be studying the aggregate to understand the current state of education. We will invite you to consider whether this understanding is an accurate reflection of your experience of school and to reflect on what actions, if any, we should take as a country, as schools, as teachers, and as parents. The aggregate serves an important purpose for all of those who care about education. However, while comparing one particular school to the aggregate can be interesting, it is not always helpful. There are two reasons for this.

First, the 8 Conditions are ideals, not norms. By testing a significant number of students, we may be able to obtain the normative level of literacy for eighth graders or the normative level of skill in numeracy for eleventh graders. We could then use that normative level as a yardstick to assess how a particular student or school compares in relationship to the norm. But the 8 Conditions are not norms; they represent ideal states. Consider for a moment what the "normative level" of Belonging would be in the seventh grade. What would it mean to say that "We are above the norm for our students having Confidence to Take Action?" We want *every* student to feel as if they belong. Every student should feel a sense of confidence. We should not be satisfied that a slightly lower percentage of our students are bored in school than the national average. As ideals, the "normative" level for each condition is 100%. As ideals, we may never attain the 100% we seek, yet we should never stop trying to attain it.

## COMMIT TO A DIRECTION

- Use student data to inform teaching.
- Share student voice data with colleagues to gain their insights.
- Invite students to share their thoughts and opinions during staff meetings.
- Allow students to interview potential new teachers and administrators.
- Include student data in personal evaluations, as well as accreditation and state reports. ■

Second, the aggregate is an abstraction. There is no such school that has nearly 57,000 students in it and a perfect 50/50 gender breakdown. When numbers are aggregated from numerous particular data sets, all the characteristics that make the particular data sets unique wash out. Many of these characteristics have a profound influence on the 8 Conditions: teacher-to-student ratio, socioeconomic status, availability of co-curricular activities, vitality of student leadership, urban, rural, or suburban setting, to name just a few. Everything that makes a school unique is missing in the aggregate. Comparing particular schools to an aggregate is not like comparing apples to oranges; it's like comparing apples to fruit juice.

The most illuminating and helpful comparisons for an individual school are internal. What do boys in a school say as compared to girls? If there is a discrepancy, what accounts for it? Is the gap acceptable? What is happening from grade level to grade level? Do different races of students report different experiences of school? If a school has taken the staff survey, do staff report different perceptions of the same indicator from the students? Are there similarities? Why?

Even absent the comparison data from the staff survey, discrepancies between students' perceptions of school and the staff's anecdotal perceptions of school can create a fruitful tension for change. On My Voice surveys, we have found a fairly big gap in perception when just 55% of students believe teachers care about them as individuals, while nearly all teachers say they care about students. When we discuss this gap with teachers, they relate how hard they work, how carefully they plan lessons, and how they correct tests and papers in a timely fashion. When we bring these efforts to the attention of students, they say that is a teacher's job, it's what they get paid to do, and that it doesn't mean teachers care. On more than one occasion, we have heard students use the term *paycheck teacher* to describe a teacher they believe is motivated solely by money. What students consider care from a teacher are all those interactions teachers have with students that are part of the unwritten job description of teaching. In our experience, the internal comparison of teachers' perceptions and student perceptions motivates change, not comparisons with an aggregate.

## Driven to Fidelity

There are two expressions in current educational jargon we do not understand: "data-driven decision making" and "implement with fidelity." Data are inanimate objects and cannot "drive" anything. And implementing a program exactly as it was drawn up in an ivory tower or by a curriculum committee, with no consideration to real conditions on the ground, is frequently an exercise in frustration, not fidelity. These two phrases suggest that those professionals most responsible for student success should take their own thinking out of the process.

The professional educators who work with students in schools every day—teachers and administrators and other school personnel—must be invited to exercise their professional judgment as they make decisions and implement programs. If you are a policymaker, curriculum designer, or program developer, we have news for you: They are doing that anyway.

The fact of the matter is that schools are different, and students are unique; there is no one-size-fits-all solution that either the data or remote decision makers could use to drive a successful outcome.

A school might also compare survey results to its mission statement or core beliefs. Provided a school lives its mission statement (see Corso, Lucey, & Fox, 2012), those analyzing survey results may want to ask: Does the school profess the centrality of community? How does that compare with what students say about Belonging? Does the mission statement espouse the importance of actively engaging students in the learning process? If so, is this reflected in the data having to do with Fun & Excitement, Curiosity & Creativity, and Spirit of Adventure?

Do the school's core beliefs highlight the value of teaching students to be productive citizens? Do the results for Confidence to Take Action bear out this emphasis?

The importance of considering survey results in light of conditions within the school itself can be illustrated with the following example. A school receives its student data and the percentages around Engagement are low. Students really are not challenging themselves, and they give up when schoolwork becomes too difficult. The gut reaction of most teachers is to jump to action since these numbers are "low." As the school digs deeper with the staff and students, together they realize that the school has been putting forth amazing efforts in areas of engagement. Students are being challenged to think creatively, and teachers strive to make learning relevant. This change in pedagogy is remarkable, yet the unanticipated side effect is that students are not yet comfortable taking risks in this new learning environment. Students who have never failed are experiencing "failure"—not in the literal sense of failing classes; rather, they have to try multiple times or simply think differently to find an answer. This particular set of student data should be used to inform the school's next steps around Engagement. They are not a reason for alarm, panic, or even immediate action.

These same principles of comparing internally apply to looking at the staff and parent surveys, as well. The bottom line is that as educators and policymakers strive for all students to reach their academic promise, they must ask: How can students meet high academic standards if they do not believe in their ability to do so? How can they learn if they are not academically engaged? How can they set and reach academic goals if they do not see the purpose in doing so? If students are to enjoy academic, social, and personal success, they must believe in themselves, be engaged in their learning, and see the connection between what they learn today and who they want to become tomorrow. When these experiences are present, academic achievement flourishes.

## IGNORANCE OF REALITY IS THE ENEMY

When focusing solely on academic outcomes as measured by standardized tests, and using these as the only data that drives decision making, schools operate out of four blind spots. Such an approach:

1. Is too constrictive given the actual breadth of outcomes schools seek to achieve.

2. Runs counter to calls that schools must educate the "whole child."

3. Does not recognize or ask schools to be accountable for the personal, social, and environmental factors that contribute to academic success.

4. Is seemingly ignorant of the fact that most students do not drop out of school or do poorly in school due to a lack of academic capacity.

Everyone working in schools knows that a successful day, week, semester, or year has outcomes that both include and go beyond the academic. Every classroom teacher knows that in order for students to be successful academically, we must employ methods that engage students' bodies and emotions and not just their brains. Every educator knows that students achieve more academically when they feel safe, when they believe we care about them, and when we recognize them for what they are already good at. Everyone who has ever tried to keep a student engaged in class knows that the biggest obstacle is not intellectual ability; it is feeling like an outsider, or being bored, or not seeing the relevance of what the class is doing. And yet, the narrowly academic accountability systems we use in schools have become the very sand into which we bury our heads.

## OVERCOME OBSTACLES

**Our evaluation system is based on student test scores, not student perception surveys.** Aspirations is one of many paths to higher test scores. Research points to the fact that there are nonacademic means to academic ends. Your own experience probably has taught you that students work harder for teachers they respect and who they believe care about them. Nor are improved test scores the only goal of schooling. We have never come across a single mission statement that professes a school's reason for existence is to raise standardized test scores as high as possible. Instead, most mission statements talk about educating the whole child and the importance of citizenship and life-long learning. Are we living our mission or someone else's (see Corso et al., 2012)?

**Student perspective is unrealistic.** Clearly students have not had as many experiences as adults. Nonetheless, no one knows their world better than they do. Students are the absolute experts in their own point of view. We must realize that our past is *not* their future. Our past experiences in school as students are far different from theirs. Students can teach us: What it means to be a student at this school (most teachers attended a different school from their students), what it means to be a student at this time (most teachers attended school a long time ago), and what it means to be them (students may have different experiences, insights, judgments, values, etc., from their teachers).

**Teachers don't take student opinions seriously.** Interestingly, the majority of students agree that teachers are not willing to learn from students (QISA, 2013). We must break that culture of "teacher knows best." Everyone takes their own opinions with the utmost seriousness. How strange then not to consider others' opinions of equal value. Teachers want their opinions and feelings heard and understood. Why don't we think students want the same thing? ∎

The result of measuring only academic ends is to remain in the dark about the means. The solutions such myopia evokes are themselves myopically academic: better reading programs, more homework in math, writing across the curriculum, and so on. To a person with a hammer, everything looks like a nail. We cancel recess so there can be more time for reading. We do away with art classes in order to expand math classes. Such solutions are deceptive because they appear to work. Test scores go up slightly in the short term, but one must squarely face whether or not improved test scores reflect genuine mastery of the material or an improved ability to take standardized tests. And one must face the question of whether this short-term pay-off is worth the long-term price of disengagement and a failure to instill a love of life-long learning.

This issue shows up at three levels. First, at the level of the individual student, we must ask whether helping students become better test takers really helps them master what we are asking them to learn. Mastery requires more than the facility for efficiently processing information, which makes for good test taking. Really understanding something, being able to probe material and ask intelligent questions about it, not just being able to answer questions, and being able to apply what one has learned, are outcomes difficult to measure with an optical mark reader. Recently, while talking to students in a state where the graduation test is in the tenth grade, a group of juniors voiced that they were genuinely mystified as to why they had to come to school for two more years, having already passed the test. More than one educational pundit has quipped that standardized testing leads to standardized teaching, which leads to standardized learning, which leads to standardized thinking. We must ask and honestly answer whether this is what our current educational system is actually producing, and whether standardized thinking fits our call to teach students 21st century skills.

Second, at the school and district levels, we have to be aware of, and accountable to, the connection between high-stakes testing and the dropout rate (Clarke, Haney, & Madaus, 2000). A school's test scores improve as bad test takers are filtered out by schooling methods that seek only to raise test scores. Inner-city schools with large populations of high-poverty students are particularly susceptible to this double-bind, as they are likely to be under pressure to make huge gains on standardized achievement markers or else be closed or taken over (see Sterns & Glennie, 2006). In a do-or-die scramble to raise scores and keep their doors open, they remove the very elements from which their struggling students could benefit most—positive relationships with teachers, classroom strategies that keep them excited and engaged in school, and a clear sense of the purpose of school in a world in which information is widely accessible. We are not calling for lowered expectations in our high-poverty schools, but rather making the case that relentlessly demanding and working for high test scores will not yield the kind of educated, bright young people that our society both desires and needs.

Third, the sheer number of tests—formative assessments, benchmarks, end-of-unit tests, end-of-course exams, summative assessments—seems verging on being out of control. In addition to how much time teachers bemoan that testing takes away from instruction, there is an inevitable impact on student engagement. As our friends in Montana quip, "You can't fatten a cow by weighing it every day!"

## When Not to Survey

In our current quest to measure everything that breathes, we may be losing sight of the big picture. We are the first to admit one should do all he or she can to get input from students and staff about the school. Obviously, one of the easiest ways to do this is in the form of a survey.

A few years ago, I was talking with a principal who was passionate about making sure her staff had a voice in her school. She was desperate to have a survey to measure her staff's perception of the effectiveness of communication in her building. After a great deal of discussion, I was really pleased to see her commitment to learning what her staff was thinking and whether or not she really had a communication issue at her school. About 20 minutes into the conversation, I innocently asked, "How many staff members are at your school?"

She said, "Six."

I asked for clarity, "Did you say 60?"

"No," she repeated, "I said six, S-I-X."

To say I was shocked is an understatement. I then said, "You don't need a survey to measure if there is a communication issue. If you only have six staff members and you think you need a survey to find out if communication is an issue, trust me, there is one!" The moral of the story is, even though collecting data is important to learn about your organization and grow, in some instances, you don't need a survey—just a little common sense.

*—RJQ*

Successful schools recognize that the best teachers, curricula, and teaching strategies available only work to the degree to which students are connected to them. This requires formative assessments, not just of learners within the classroom, but also of the classroom and school as a learning environment. It requires tools that not only measure the academic outcomes we are hoping to achieve, but that also assess the various means we are using to get there. It's as if the only number we care about on a road trip is the GPS coordinates that will say we have arrived, but what about the gas gauge, the tire pressure, the oil light, and the engine temperature?

We must discover whether our students believe in themselves, because students who believe in themselves work harder academically. We must discover whether they are engaged by the experiences we are providing for them, because students who are meaningfully engaged learn more deeply, as well as learn *how* to learn. We must discover what they think our expectations of them are, because children rise or fall to our expectations, both academically and behaviorally. We must discover whether they see any purpose in what we are asking them to learn, because students who see a purpose in what they are learning pursue it with greater intensity. As long as we remain ignorant of these vital factors, we run the risk of employing solutions that may work in the short run but do great harm down the road.

## Lost 45s

Sometimes, when I am standing in front of a classroom of students explaining why student voice is so important to schools trying to be successful, I will hold up a small, 1½ inch yellow disc that resembles a spiral arm galaxy and ask if they know what it is. None do. Sometimes, even the newer teachers are stumped. A game piece? A kind of paper clip? Those of a certain generation know that this is an insert that allowed people to put vinyl records known as 45s (sometimes I have to explain what they are, too) on a turntable with a spindle so that they could drop down for listening. Imagine being able to listen to five songs in a row without having to get up!

I go on to narrate the history of my access to music for the past 40 years from vinyl to 8 tracks (portable music!) to cassettes (Sony Walkman!) to CDs to iTunes. I conclude by saying that although my current iPod contains my entire music collection, I rarely listen to it because—I take out my iPhone—I listen to music on my phone/Internet/calculator/computer/camera/game thing.

The way I access music has changed five times since I was in middle school. And yet most middle and high school classrooms today look exactly like my middle and high school classrooms. Music hasn't changed (well, the music I listen to hasn't changed), nor have my ears (yet), but the way I access music has changed dramatically. The nature of knowledge hasn't changed and brains are still brains, but the way we interact with knowledge has to change if education is going to be relevant, engaging, and purposeful for our students. Absent student voice, the current state of education is like trying to play a 45 on a smartphone. Even the yellow disc won't help.

—MJC

# Listening Broadly

The information contained in the My Voice results is invaluable. We have only begun to mine this data for insights into our schools and our students' experiences. As you will see, the message is very clear: For about half the students in this country, school works. It meets their intellectual, emotional, and social needs. Their Self-Worth is fostered, they experience Engagement, and they are developing a sense of Purpose. But for the other half of students, school does not work at all.

The findings from My Voice are replicated in several other surveys that have parallel concerns and a similarly national reach. Indiana University's Center for Evaluation and Education Policy administered its High School Survey of Student Engagement from 2003–13. In its most recent national publication of results, only 57% of students agree that "I am an important part of my high school community." Nearly half of students (49%) indicated they are bored every day. Students were asked on the survey, "Why do you go to school?" Regarding the purpose of school, Yazzie-Mintz, the study's author, writes, "The assumption can be made that students only go to school because they are required" (2009, p. 5). Gallup's Student Survey measures Well Being, Engagement, and Hopefulness—categories that parallel the 3 Guiding Principles of Self-Worth, Engagement, and Purpose. Its 2013 results for each category

are 66%, 55%, and 54%, respectively (Gallup, 2013). As with My Voice over the years, these studies are remarkably consistent across the research world: School works for half of students and does not work for the other half.

In terms of the Aspirations Framework, far too many students do not believe they belong in school and have too few heroes in school. School does not recognize what they are good at, does not seem relevant to what they are interested in, and is not a place that invites their creativity or curiosity. They are unwilling to take the risks necessary to learn out of fear of failure, or even out of fear of success. They believe they have little say in any of what goes on, and they move from class to class just to get through. Some in this group indeed do *not* get through; they drop out. This reality is not the enemy. We must take to heart what these students are telling us if we hope to have the passion necessary to improve our schools.

# ARRIVE

In schools that effectively use student voice data:

- Students regularly complete surveys and focus groups.
- Students present their data at board meetings and staff meetings.
- Teachers use student data to inform classroom decisions.
- Teachers use student perspective to inform their teaching.
- Administrators consider student data as part of teacher evaluation.
- Administrators seek student input into their performance. ■

CHAPTER 4

# Students Speak About Self-Worth

*I like this school because I get to hang out with friends, and I love my teacher; it's like she's my friend. I just love school so much!*

—second-grade female student

*A teacher might look at you and think you're bad, but you ain't.*

—seventh-grade male student

Students who have Self-Worth are more likely to have high aspirations (Osterman, 2000, p. 328; see also Erikson, 1963; Markus & Nurius, 1986; Nurmi, 1991). Though they are frequently synonymous, we chose the term "self-worth" over "self-esteem" to emphasize that the goal is for students to believe in their worth and value, not just feel good about themselves. We have met students who feel good about themselves but lacked real confidence in their own worth and abilities. Conversely, we have met young people who have a basic confidence in their value and believe in their abilities but struggle with feeling good about who they are. As much as we hope the two go together, what counts most for having high aspirations is believing in yourself, knowing that you are of value for being the unique person you are. Developing self-worth in students is the responsibility of *everyone* working in a school, whereas developing self-esteem may be the responsibility of school counselors and psychologists.

The path to Self-Worth begins with our relationships. We learn to value ourselves when others value us. This is because relationships and community precede the individual. It may seem as if we are first self-reliant individuals who then form bonds with one another called relationships. However, before there is an "I," there is a "we."

49

Self-Worth is not at first a self-generated reality: instead we begin to develop Self-Worth based on the extent to which we internalize others' acceptance of who we are. This, of course, begins in the family and continues within the school community.

## ■ ■ ■ ASSESS YOUR STARTING POINT

Use the best practices for supporting student self-worth below to rate yourself on a scale of 0-10, where 0 is never and 10 is always.

- I treat students as individuals who have unique skills and talents.

- I welcome and solicit divergent opinions and ideas.

- I know my students' strengths and challenges.

- I greet students as they enter my classes.

- My students know I respect them as individuals.

- I am a positive role model for my students.

- My students create portfolios to represent their best work.

- Students know I value hard work and persistence. ■

In a school setting, the same chronological priority of relationship before individuality exists. Before any particular child walks into a school, there exists the general relationship of teacher-student. How teachers and students understand that general relationship (e.g., expert-novice, possessor of information-blank slate, co-learners) shapes each unique, particular relationship, and helps define what the individuals bring to their relationship. For example, if a teacher views learning as reciprocal among teachers and students, her pupils will have much to teach her. But if a teacher does not believe she has anything to learn from students, no individual student, no matter how insightful, will be able to teach her. These general beliefs about school-based relationships help shape the Conditions associated with building students' Self-Worth.

## Infrequent Flyer

On a recent return trip from across The Pond, I heard a statement from a 5-year-old that really struck a chord with me. I was standing in Heathrow airport, Gate 14, and boarding was about to begin. A young boy standing nearby was scared and clearly did not want to get on the plane. Despite the kind words and gentle coaxing from his mother, he would not budge. After several attempts and no progress, his mom became frustrated and said, "Okay. Knock it off. Everyone flies!" Without a moment's hesitation, the boy looked right up at her and said, "I am not everyone. I am me." In a single moment, a 5-year-old boy captured my life's work and the Quaglia Institute for Student Aspirations' philosophy about working with kids.

That young boy could not have cared less if *everyone* flies. He just knew that flying was not for him. The power of those words, "I am not everyone, I am *me*" should echo in the minds of all educators as we work to teach students in schools that are understaffed, classes that are overcrowded, and with content that, frankly, at times can be a bit boring. It is incumbent on us to remember that our classes are composed of students with individual minds, thoughts, feelings, and beliefs. There is no such person as "everyone."

And in case you're curious . . . the inspiration for this reflection, the young boy at Heathrow, did get on the plane. In fact, he sat in the seat directly behind me yelling and kicking my seat for the duration of the flight, adding a five-hour exclamation point to his statement at the gate!

—*RJQ*

Primary to developing Self-Worth among students is the Condition of Belonging or what is sometimes referred to as "connectedness" (see National Research Council of Medicine, 2004, pp. 33–34). This is fostered in school when a student can be part of the school community and yet maintain his or her individuality. Belonging depends, at a minimum, on feeling safe and comfortable in school. In such a school, students are not put down or bullied for being different. Rather, differences are perceived as making the school community *stronger*. Beyond feeling safe, Self-Worth develops when students genuinely feel welcomed and appreciated, and when others in the community consider their feelings and concerns. When students are accepted in this way, they develop an attachment to the community that is often expressed as pride.

Self-Worth is further developed when a student has another person in his or her life who respects, supports, and cares for him or her unconditionally. We describe this using the term *Hero*. Here we see again the importance of relationships to Self-Worth (see Osterman, 2000, p. 328). Whereas Belonging deals with the relationship between the individual and a community, the Condition of Heroes focuses on the relationship between two individuals. To build belief in herself, a student must have a particular person who actively believes in her—someone who "champions" her value. To have Self-Worth, a student must experience herself as worthwhile in another's eyes. Again, for most of us this experience comes first in the family and extends to others as we engage in school and neighborhood communities.

In a school setting, there are a variety of people who can serve as Heroes. Teachers, because they make up the majority of a school's personnel, and because they have the most interactions with students, bear a tremendous responsibility to care for and relate to students in a way that nurtures their Self-Worth. Teachers who are available to their students, show them genuine respect, and care about them as individuals, not just as students, help students recognize their value. We hear all the time from students that, second to their parents, teachers are everyday Heroes in their lives. In addition to teachers who serve as Heroes, administrators, coaches, guidance counselors, support staff, and even other students can all provide the respect and care necessary to develop Self-Worth.

## REFLECT ON YOUR SURROUNDINGS

- How do you learn and incorporate individual student's interests, hobbies, and aspirations?

- What do students think is respectful behavior from their teachers?

- When you see disrespectful interactions between teachers and students, what do you do?

- What difference does it make if you allow students the opportunity to improve and revise their work?

- What can you do to ensure that student report cards reflect more than just a letter grade? ■

Last, Self-Worth is engendered when a student is recognized and celebrated for his effort, perseverance, good citizenship, and a diversity of accomplishments. This form of recognition, what we term Sense of Accomplishment, is distinct from being recognized for what one has "done" or produced. Sense of Accomplishment emphasizes value located *within* the self, rather than externally in an outcome the self has brought about. This distinction is subtle, but important. The independent, inner experience of a student believing herself to be valuable begins when the worth others recognize is *in* her, in the inwardly generated effort and perseverance she put into the work to produce an outcome. Similarly, when a student is recognized for being kind or helpful to another, it is the kindness *in* him that is referenced along with the kind act itself. These inwardly generated harbingers of success—effort, perseverance, kindness—are part of what Carol Dweck (2006) refers to as a "growth mindset" as distinct from a "fixed mindset." When students learn to attach success to variables within their control—how hard they work, how long they study, and so on—they are more likely to be successful. Schools can foster a growth mindset by recognizing and celebrating these inner drives.

## COMMIT TO A DIRECTION

- Regularly inquire about students' activities outside of school.

- Share your own personal (not private!) experiences with students.

- Place photographs of your family and friends in your classroom and around your desk.

- Ask at least two students a day how they are doing, and wait for a response.

- Attend student events—especially the ones that are not so popular.

- Acknowledge different types of achievement and accomplishments (i.e., being polite, kind, courteous, showing a little extra effort).

- Provide opportunities for students to be involved in community service activities both in and outside of school.

- Require all students to develop academic, personal, and social goals. ◾

Similarly, when others note some skill or talent that is innate to a student—for some this is academic, for others athletic, for others artistic, and so on—the locus of worth is internal. While talent may be more "fixed" than effort and perseverance, still a student can choose to develop a talent or not. Developing a talent that seems undervalued by one's school community may seem like a waste of time, and so many students with a talent for dance or music or comedy put their energies elsewhere. To support the Self-Worth of all students, students must be recognized and celebrated by others for what is inside them—effort, kindness, and talent.

## OVERCOME OBSTACLES

**I teach too many students to know them as individuals.** It is impossible to teach well without knowing your students. Realize that when you do not take the time to know each student as an individual, they are not learning to their potential. Simply knowing a student's hopes and dreams will have a profound impact in connecting with him or her in the classroom.

**I don't want to be my students' hero.** Let's be clear. It is not up to the teacher if he or she wishes to be a hero to students. It is up to the students. No adult in a school gets to walk up to a

*(Continued)*

(Continued)

student and say "I'm going to be your hero today." And no adult working in a school gets to walk away from a student saying, "Sorry, kid, I'm not going to be your hero today." A teacher's only choice in the matter is if he or she chooses to be a good hero or not. Never underestimate the influence you have on students—whether you want it or not.

**Our report cards are dictated by the school board or central office.** For too long, we have accepted the fact that report cards are the only way we can document and share student growth. The fact that your school uses traditional report cards does not preclude anyone from offering richer forms of feedback to students and parents. Create meaningful ways for students to demonstrate their personal, social, and academic progress. Have your students develop portfolios, journals, and personal reflections that can be shared with their parents. Let students know that their effort, perseverance, and citizenship really do matter. ∎

In schools, we tend to recognize and celebrate academic (and in some schools, athletic) "end-product" more so than the effort and perseverance that went into producing them. Academic output in the form of grades is often given pride of place on report cards, while the column for effort, if it exists, seems an afterthought. Yet a teacher who applauds the effort put in to raising a C– to a B does more for a student's Self-Worth than the Honors certificate the B makes the student eligible to receive. Students do not need to be in school for very long to know that As and

Bs have a value. The question for Self-Worth is whether students are valued for who they are, more so than for what they produce in the way of academic outcomes (Dweck, 2006).

These three factors—being a part of a community while being valued for one's uniqueness, having someone who cares for and respects one as one is, and being recognized for one's effort, perseverance, good citizenship, and talents—contribute profoundly to one's sense of Self-Worth. These factors comprise the first three Conditions of Belonging, Heroes, and Sense of Accomplishment and are the Conditions that need to be in place if our students are to develop the Self-Worth necessary to set and achieve their goals. Let's turn to the survey results and examine what students have to say about Belonging, Heroes, and Sense of Accomplishment in their schools.

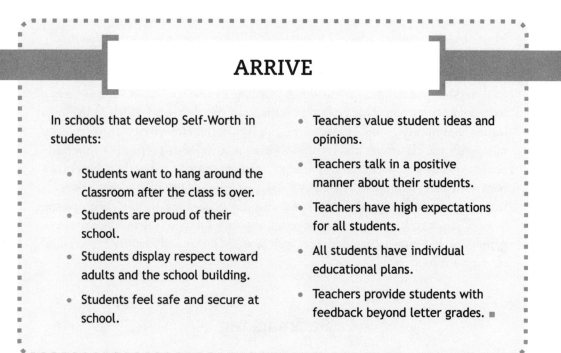

## ARRIVE

In schools that develop Self-Worth in students:

- Students want to hang around the classroom after the class is over.
- Students are proud of their school.
- Students display respect toward adults and the school building.
- Students feel safe and secure at school.

- Teachers value student ideas and opinions.
- Teachers talk in a positive manner about their students.
- Teachers have high expectations for all students.
- All students have individual educational plans.
- Teachers provide students with feedback beyond letter grades. ■

## CONDITION 1: BELONGING

*One of the things I like about our school is that there are cliques, but they are not set in stone. Just because you hang out with one group of students doesn't mean you can't be with another group. If the table where you normally eat lunch is full, you can sit at another table and it's cool.*

—tenth-grade female student

*I feel happy because they actually greet you at the door. And on the first day of school I was kind of nervous.*

—third-grade female student

Have you ever seen a student walk into a room and struggle to belong, an experience where you could immediately sense he was not welcome and might be better off turning around? Or can you think of a time when a student added important diversity to a group, diversity of background, perspective, or interests, and was valued for it? It does not take long to realize, when we reflect upon our own experiences, that students are more likely to thrive academically, socially, and emotionally if they feel they belong at school (Klem & Connell, 2005). Vitally important to true Belonging is that students can retain, and be appreciated for, their uniqueness, even as they participate within the larger school community.

More than 50 years ago, John Dewey made the case that education is essentially the creation of experiences that lead to learning, and that since the development of experience comes about through social interaction, social interactions warrant considerable pedagogical attention. According to Dewey, "Education is essentially a social process. This quality is realized in the degree in which individuals form a community group" (1938, p. 58). Educators, therefore, have a responsibility to manage the classroom and common spaces in a way that promotes connectedness as well as a responsibility to interact with students in a way that shows they personally care. More recent studies show that "the quality of students' relationships with adults and peers in the home and school, and specifically, their perceptions of support, have important connections with levels of intrinsic motivation, autonomy, and internal regulation as well as self-esteem and identity integration" (Osterman, 2000, p. 328).

# Backpacking

In response to students indicating that they did not feel their school was a welcoming and friendly place, one class of elementary students decided to take action. A group of self-designated leaders began by interviewing classmates and asking, "What makes you feel welcomed at school?" This particular school had a highly transient population. The students learned that newcomers frequently felt lost and scared when they came to school.

In response, the students decided to put together New Student Backpacks. They wrote a proposal and submitted it to several local businesses. Businesses came forward to buy the backpacks, as well as school supplies to put in the backpacks. For the students' part, they designed school maps, copied lunch menus, and provided a list of "Helpful Things to Know." The latter contained important information that the adults sometimes overlooked like: the custodian's name is Mr. Humphrey; if you ask, the lunch lady will give you an extra milk; and the chain on the middle swing in the playground can pinch your hand.

The students, not the adults, developed all the contents for the backpack. They even put together a "Welcome to our School" DVD. Prior to entering the school, new students could watch the DVD and take a virtual tour of the school. The student leaders even created buttons that read, "Ask Me for Help" so any new student knew whom to approach if they were lost or had questions.

There are two key aspects to the condition of Belonging in schools. First, at the communal level, a school environment should be warm, welcoming, and friendly. Students must perceive school as a place they feel connected and supported. Students should be safe from unwelcome behaviors, like bullying, and feel comfortable in common areas. Additionally, a school to which a student feels he or she belongs is a source of pride. Second, at a more personal level, students should feel accepted for who they are by teachers and peers, and believe that teachers care about their problems and feelings. The following My Voice statements test for these two indicators of school Belonging:

| BELONGING STATEMENTS | % IN AGREEMENT |
| --- | --- |
| School is a welcoming and friendly place. | 66% |
| I feel accepted for who I am at school. | 72% |
| Teachers make an effort to get to know me. | 57% |
| I have difficulty fitting in at school. | 21% |
| Teachers care about my problems and feelings. | 51% |
| I am proud of my school. | 58% |
| I am a valued member of my school community. | 45% |
| I think bullying is a problem in my school. | 49% |

Clearly, far too many students do not experience school as a place they feel a sense of connection, pride, support, and safety. These findings may surprise teachers and school leaders who work to create a sense of community within the school building. While nearly three quarters of students agree with the statement "I feel accepted for who I am at school," the finding that only about half of the students surveyed believe their teachers care about their problems and feelings is troubling. While most teachers would claim they care deeply about their students, teachers need to express their care in ways that are meaningful for students. For many students, this is as much about teachers'

interest in them at a personal level (e.g., inquiring about hobbies outside of school, attending sports events or theatrical performances) as it is about teachers preparing lessons and correcting assignments in a timely fashion. When we ask students about these latter efforts as evidence that teachers care, students reply, "I want teachers to care about *me*, not just my grades."

When a student feels valued for who he is, his experience of school, in general, is more positive. Promoting Belonging and community is a value in its own right, but in a school we must be well aware of the impact that feeling part of the community has on the learning environment. In a review of research that shows the impact of Belonging on academic outcomes, Osterman notes that "students who experienced a greater sense of acceptance by peers and teachers were more likely to be interested in and enjoy school and their classes. These perceptions of school were also reflected in their commitment to their work, higher expectations of success, and lower levels of anxiety" (2000, p. 331).

# Home Work

When they began Aspirations work, teachers at a middle school in the southern United States with a high-poverty population devised a plan to increase their students' sense of Belonging. While the teachers knew that they wanted to increase belonging *within* the school, they felt that their efforts to do so would need to extend *beyond* the building's walls. Many admitted that they did not know enough about what students' lives were really like outside of school, and so they came up with a variety of ways to participate in their students' community, each of which provided important new perspectives.

Home visits helped forge positive relationships between teachers and their students' families, which led parents to feel increasingly more welcome at the school. Attending their church services furthered the growing sense of community between teachers and families and inspired new instructional techniques, such as call and response, that excited and engaged their learners. A rotating schedule at the beginning of the school year provided teachers with the opportunity to ride on their students' buses and experience firsthand what the first 40 minutes of "school" was like for them. On a curriculum level, they changed reading lists to include books that more accurately reflected students' lives and interests, and incorporated more African American and Hispanic heroes in their lessons and wall displays. Their efforts helped the school flourish. Among their accomplishments, teachers felt most proud of the fact that students and their families felt new ownership of the school. They had not only increased their students' belonging in school, but also they had increased the school's belonging within the community, as well.

## IMPROVING THE ODDS

In addition to these general results, we are going to look more deeply into each of these statements using an odds analysis.[1] Simply stated, the question our odds

---

[1] All odds analysis statistics throughout this book reflect the results of analyses known as logistic regressions, which allow for the prediction of agreement with one statement based on the proportion of

analysis answers is, "If students agree with a particular statement, what is the likelihood that they will agree with another particular statement on the survey?" This allows us to describe the relationship between statements that are indicative of a certain Condition (like Belonging), to learn if they have an effect on students' academic effort or engagement. In this way, we can be confident that if we work on improving students' experience of the first statement, the odds increase that they will also improve the second statement.

72% of students agree that "I feel accepted for who I am at school." These students are . . .

- 8 times more likely to believe they can be successful
- 4 times more likely to say they enjoy being at school
- 4 times more likely to agree they enjoy participating in classes
- 4 times more likely to report they feel comfortable asking questions in class
- 3 times more likely to say they learn new things that are interesting to them at school
- 3 times more likely to believe what they learn in school will benefit their future
- 3 times more likely to say they put forth their best effort at school
- 3 times more likely to indicate they push themselves to do better academically

. . . than those who do not agree that they feel accepted for who they are.

As Anderman has noted, the relationship between belonging and academic outcomes is reciprocal in nature (2003). Students who feel connected to school do better academically, and doing better academically helps students feel more connected to school. One finding of the study is that "students who perceive their classes as task and goal oriented reported higher levels of belonging than did others" (Anderman, 2003, p. 17). Teachers who feel that it is beyond the scope of their job description to nurture a social environment in which students feel connected to their school can trust that choosing educational strategies that are collaborative and task and goal oriented may be as effective in promoting Belonging as ice-breakers, using students' names, or other get-to-know-you sessions.

agreement with another statement. All of these results were statistically significant. All such analyses statistically controlled for grade level, gender, race, and school; this suggests that independent of each of these factors, the odds results are meaningful. All figures have been rounded up or down to the nearest whole number.

**51% of students agree that "Teachers care about my problems and feelings. These students are . . .**

- 7 times more likely to believe that teachers recognize them when they try their best
- 7 times more likely to agree that teachers help them learn from their mistakes
- 7 times more likely to feel that teachers encourage students to make decisions
- 6 times more likely to say that teachers make school an exciting place to learn
- 5 times more likely to indicate they are encouraged to be creative

**. . . than those who did not agree that teachers care about their problems and feelings.**

While some teachers may be uncomfortable showing students they care about them at this personal level, most would agree that effort, emotional investment, creativity, learning from mistakes, and practice in decision making have a positive impact on learning and academic achievement. One very concrete effect that feeling accepted can have on the learning environment is discerned in an odds ratio result of the statement "I feel comfortable asking questions in class." Few educators would dispute the importance of asking questions in the classroom in order to improve learning and uncover gaps in a student's understanding. Students who agreed with the statement "I feel accepted for who I am at school" are nearly four times more likely to agree with the statement "I feel comfortable asking questions in class." As educators, we know how challenging it can be for students to reveal their lack of understanding by asking a question in class, and in focus groups we often hear students confirm this fear. Creating an emotionally safe environment is vital to questioning, which is in turn vital to learning.

Teachers, in particular, can have a profound effect on a student's experience of school, to the extent that students perceive teachers caring about them as more than as "just another student." Students who agreed with the statement "Teachers care about my problems and feelings" were seven times more likely to agree that teachers recognize their best efforts, that teachers help them learn from their mistakes, and that teachers encourage them to make decisions. They were also six times more likely to feel teachers make school an exciting place to learn and five times more likely to say teachers encourage them to be creative.

To support the condition of Belonging, teachers must be willing to do three simple things. *First*, learn students' names and use them. That sounds simple; however, we work in many schools where the student population is wonderfully diverse. Student names are not John, Sue, and Mark. Rather names include Dez'meon, Na'Quaisia, and Ra'Quan. Mispronouncing a name may not seem like a big deal; however, it relays the message to the student that he or she is not important as an individual. We are sensitive to how many student names a teacher may need to get to know, and yet we are also aware of the effect that "sweetheart" and "honey" have on students. We were in one school and the teacher had given all students a prompt related to the first month of school. One student wrote, "I have really enjoyed school so far. Your class is interesting and I am working hard to learn what you are teaching. I wish you would work as hard at learning how to say my name." It mattered to this student.

*Second*, teachers must know their students' interests and dreams. Making learning relevant for students is nearly impossible unless you know them. We don't expect everything that happens in a classroom to relate to every student's aspiration; however, when teachers make even a minimal effort to connect learning to students' interests and dreams, students feel more connected. One teacher we know had students create a personal aspirations Wordle and made them a permanent feature of her classroom. These were a reminder for her to stay connected to her students by referencing relevant associations as they came up. Although knowing students is a challenge when many teachers have well over a hundred students, it is no less a challenge to effectively teach students you don't know.

*Third*, and perhaps the easiest way a teacher can promote Belonging is to greet students when they enter the room. Don't shuffle papers behind the desk, calibrate the interactive whiteboard, or hassle students about dress code before they even sit down. Stand at the door, look your students in the eye, say "Good morning" or "Good afternoon" and let them know they matter to you.

Ultimately, if we are to increase the number of students who feel connected to their school, we must ask students how they would foster a welcoming and supportive school environment. What does a welcoming school look like to students? How can the cafeteria be re-imagined so it is a place where all students feel comfortable? How do students in different grades define respect? How do boys define bullying differently than girls? If we listen to the voices of students as to how they define the condition of Belonging, and take action based on those findings, we will, in that very process, be connecting students more deeply to school.

— ᏣᎨᎤ —

## CONDITION 2: HEROES

*For certain I would like all teachers to know more about me—the one teacher that I have that relationship with, I strive for; he seems to view us as friends and colleagues not just as students. I can't wait to get to that class.*

—tenth-grade male student

*I love my teacher. She is so nice and funny.*

—kindergarten male student

If you were like us, one of the best things about being a kid at the beginning of the school year was getting a few new things—jeans, sneakers, and best of all: a new lunchbox. We grew up during the days when it was cool to have a metal lunchbox (and matching thermos, of course). And you guessed it—there was a superhero on the lid. While times and trends have changed for the young people entering our schools today, our kids still love a good superhero. Spiderman, Batman, and Wonder Woman continue to live on, and have been joined by such perplexing characters as the Red Power Ranger and Optimus Prime. These superheroes, and the celebrity sports, music, and movie superstars that replace them in later years, may garner much admiration from our children, but we have heard from students time and time again that the *real* heroes in their lives are the people who care for and about them. Most significantly, young people cite their parents and their teachers as the everyday heroes who inspire them to excel as good students and citizens.

What our research shows is that, whether we know it or not—or are ready for it or not—teachers are heroes to the students they teach. As we have said, it is not up to us to decide to be a hero, but rather to determine what kind of hero we will be. Our daily decisions about how we interact with students—whether we actively listen to both students in the midst of a dispute or hastily take sides or assign blame, whether we move about the room answering students' questions or sit stalwartly at our desks checking e-mail—impact whether we will be the hero or antihero to the young people in our care.

Choosing to be a constructive force—a Hero—in students' lives is of immense value to the development of their Self-Worth, and therefore aspirations. So how are we doing? Here is what students have to say:

| HEROES STATEMENTS | % IN AGREEMENT |
| --- | --- |
| I have a teacher who is a positive role model for me. | 75% |
| Teachers care about me as an individual. | 55% |
| Teachers care if I am absent from school. | 51% |
| If I have a problem, I have a teacher with whom I can talk. | 56% |
| My parents care about my education. | 95% |
| Students respect teachers. | 41% |
| Students respect each other. | 33% |
| Teachers respect students. | 62% |

It would appear that the teacher-student relationship is tenuous for many students. Imagine being a student who believed that teachers did not care for or even respect students. While the most positive result in the above chart is that three quarters of students say they have a teacher who is a role model, the fact that students interact with so many teachers in a school year indicates that this percentage could, and should, be much higher. An average student will meaningfully encounter well over 50 adults in the course of his school career. In addition to this sheer number of encounters, students' "relationships to teachers are considered especially potent because of the many roles teachers play, for example, as a potential attachment figure, as a pedagogue, as a disciplinarian, and as the final arbiter of a student's level of performance" (Furrer & Skinner 2003, p. 150).

## Salute

A high school teacher in South Carolina recently told us this story:

There was this kid Zach; he was a sophomore in my social studies class. He always seemed to have a chip on his shoulder. He never did anything bad enough to set off the big alarms, but he was just always a little late for class, always a little too sloppy with his homework, always a little unprepared for tests, always a little too short with his temper.

I guess I am the kind of teacher some kids call "a hard ass." I try not to let kids get away with too much. So Zach and I had frequent conversations about his attitude and behavior. Once, I even told him that if he ever needed help or someone to talk to I was available. He never took me up on the offer. February of that year, he dropped out. I figured he was going to be another one of those kids that got away.

Six years later, Zach walked into my classroom in a Marine Corps uniform. He said that after he dropped out, he moved to California to be with his dad. (His parents had divorced his sophomore year.) He got back into school and eventually joined the Marines. He said he had come back to the high school just to see me. "You were the only one here who never gave up on me," he said, "and I wanted to come back to show you what I made of myself and say 'thanks.'"

Now, I have great colleagues and I am sure none of them gave up on Zach either, but I guess something in my approach, something that I said, had an impact. I had no idea how important the small, little things we do every day are. Here I am thinking I am teaching social studies, and yet what really matters happens around the edges and in the spaces of all that.

There may be an explanation, though not an excuse, for why one quarter of students cannot relate to a teacher as a positive role model. Every adult has passed through an enormous sorting system known as schooling. On the other side of numerous filters—primary and secondary school, college, graduate school—educators have chosen a career that puts them right back in school, this time on the other side of the desk. For such a role, the "filters" have selected for a love of reading, an enjoyment of learning for learning's sake, a passion for certain academic content, and a comfort level with young people.

Teachers represent just over 2% of occupations. In addition, teachers are disproportionately female and disproportionately white (Fiestritzer, 2011). Students, on the other hand, have yet to pass through the filtering system and so represent the full diversity of the general population. Some will become teachers, and some will love learning enough to complete a bachelor's degree (17%), or even a master's degree (10%). Seen in this light, that 75% of students affirm that they have a teacher who is a role model is a tribute to the effort of teachers under challenging odds.

## (On and) Off the Walls

Students working to improve the Condition of Heroes in an urban school in Ohio opted to focus on the walls.

First, they designated a corridor in the building as "The Hall of Heroes." Students brought in photos, drew pictures, and wrote stories about the people in their lives who had made a difference. They worked with the art teacher to go beyond bulletin boards to make a colorful and visually rich display of the men and women who were making a positive impact on their lives.

Second, the student leadership team became heroes themselves and inspired their peers to do likewise by confronting the graffiti and profanity issues in their building. Bothered by these ugly displays, the team decided to use their morning assemblies to draw attention to the issue. They connected their Heroes data from the My Voice survey with the problem, and asked each student to make a pledge to respect their building. As a result of these morning assemblies and a raised awareness, the graffiti and profanity issues have diminished significantly.

The key to improving this number is threefold. First, the teaching staff must reflect together on students they see falling through the cracks. Once students who do not seem to be connected to an adult in the school have been identified, willing teachers should make an effort to extend themselves to those students. Perhaps the teachers could have lunch one day in the cafeteria or inquire about the game last night—a simple, but conscious outreach, and one for which the teacher is accountable to his or her colleagues to make.

Second, we must make sure every adult working in schools is available as a role model for students. Note that we are arguing for every adult—teachers, custodians, administrators, secretaries, school volunteers, counselors, coaches, nurses—to be *available* as Heroes. The students will then choose their role models from those available. This may require some training for those who do not have a background working directly with students, but even those who do not encounter students every day in the course of their work should be enlisted if they are willing. Some of the most successful advisory programs we have seen pair a classroom teacher with a member of the nonteaching staff. Some students connect better with nonteachers.

Third, schools need programs that put students in contact with adults from outside of the school building. As the largest school board in Canada, Toronto District School Board serves a diverse population of learners. In one elementary school, the principal wanted to better connect community members with her students, as well as connect adults with children of different racial and ethnic backgrounds. The principal worked with us on developing and implementing an Aspirations Advocate Program in which community members were trained to serve as mentors to students in the school. Mentors were not matched with students based on race or ethnicity; rather, they were paired based on interests. Students who loved math were matched with adults who also enjoyed math. Likewise, sports-minded students were paired with adults who wanted to be active during the meeting times. The program was a rousing success. Time and time again the advocates would say, "I don't know why my student needs an advocate, he is perfect." Properly vetted, members of the local community (starting with the school board) should be regular visitors to every school and available as mentors to all students, but especially for those who do not see in their teacher, through no fault of the teacher, a role model.

## IMPROVING THE ODDS

The importance of students having role models is for academic as well as personal reasons. Citing several earlier studies, Furrer & Skinner write that "in early adolescence, children's feelings of teacher support predict achievement expectancies and values as well as effort, engagement, and performance" (Furrer & Skinner 2003, p. 150). Our odds analysis shows a high degree of correlation between students having teachers as role models and indicators having to do with students' perceptions of effort, grades, enjoyment in learning, and relevance.

75% of students say "I have a teacher who is a positive role model for me." These students are . . .

- 4 times more likely to say they enjoy participating in classes
- 4 times more likely to believe that learning can be fun
- 4 times more likely to say they enjoy learning new things

- 3 times more likely to feel that their classes help them understand what is happening in their everyday lives
- 3 times more likely to indicate that they put forth their best effort at school
- 3 times more likely to say that they push themselves to do better academically
- 3 times more likely to believe getting good grades is important
- 3 times more likely to report they enjoy being at school

**. . . than those who do not agree that they have a teacher who is a positive role model.**

Students who believe they have a teacher who is a positive role model are three times more likely to report putting forth their best effort at school, to push themselves to do better academically, and to consider getting good grades important than students who do not report having a teacher who is a role model. Students who find a role model among their teachers are also three times more likely to enjoy school and four times more likely to enjoy participating in their classes, to believe that learning can be fun, and to enjoy learning new things. They are also three times more likely to see the connection between what they are learning and their lives. In whatever ways make the most sense for your school, ensuring that every student has a teacher who is a positive role model can triple the odds and then some that students will find school enjoyable, meaningful, and worth putting academic effort into.

Beyond role modeling, the condition of Heroes is about being an adult who students believe cares about them, who they can trust, and who they can turn to in times of difficulty. The finding that less than half of all students surveyed perceive these characteristics in their teachers reveals an area of concern for educators. Clearly, teachers care about their students. Most teachers are underpaid, work long hours to prepare and follow-up on lessons, and even pay out of pocket for supplies they cannot obtain because of tightening school budgets. We have met and have been privileged to work beside such generous teachers. The challenge for educators is to show care in ways that students perceive care.

We have heard from students who do not believe their teachers care about them as individuals that they do believe teachers care about them as *students*—that is, as one of many. They cite as evidence for this claim the very same behaviors teachers often list as signs of care: preparing interesting lessons, correcting work in a timely fashion, arriving early and staying late. The difference is that students perceive this as a teacher's job, not as care for them personally.

Students tell us that individualized care includes asking questions about interests outside of school, inquiring about family members, attending games or performances or dropping in on practices or rehearsals, visiting with students during lunch, and being available after school for help with an assignment or just to chat. They also cite being held accountable and being challenged in a positive way as a sign that a teacher cares about them as an individual. For students, it is not just the "nice" teachers who care; it is also the "tough" teachers. Students tell us (though they may not tell their teachers) that teachers who do not let them get away with things are Heroes. According to the odds analysis, students who agreed that teachers care about them as an individual are a whopping 10 times more likely to also agree that teachers expect them to be successful.

You might anticipate a high correlation between students who think teachers care and other indicators that measure students' perceptions of their relationship with teachers: being available to talk, being recognized when they are kind and helpful, being recognized for trying their best, enjoyment in working with students, and so on. You would be right. Students who believe their teachers care about them as individuals are more likely than those who do not to view the entire relationship more favorably.

Perhaps less obvious is that students who feel cared for as individuals by their teachers are also more likely to engage in pro-academic behaviors. Such students are three times more likely to report putting forth their best effort, working hard to reach their goals, and pushing themselves to do better academically than are peers who do not report believing teachers care. They also report a higher rate of belief that school is preparing them well for their futures and are three times more likely to believe they can make a difference in the world.

**55% of students believe "Teachers care about me as an individual." These students are also . . .**

- 5 times more likely to think that what they learn in school is preparing them for their futures
- 3 times more likely to say they put forth their best effort in school
- 3 times more likely to feel they push themselves to do better academically
- 3 times more likely to report that they work hard to reach their goals
- 3 times more likely to believe they can make a difference in this world

**. . . than those who do not agree that their teachers care about them as individuals.**

These findings are supported by numerous studies. For example, in research on the application of self-determination theory in schools, Reeve concluded that "the quality of a student's motivation depends, in part, on the quality of student-teacher relationships" (2002, p. 183). He notes a particular connection between student-teacher relationships and students' engaged involvement in what they are learning. According to this study, such involvement is fostered by "the teacher's willingness to dedicate psychological resources (e.g., time, energy) to the students (e.g., expressing affection, enjoying spending time with students)" (Reeve 2002, p. 195). When students have teachers who believe in them, students believe in themselves. When they have teachers who care about them as individuals, they work harder and at least try to achieve more for themselves and for their teachers. We would argue that the payoffs to achievement are worth the price in shifting how teachers express their care for students to include a visit to a baseball practice or attending a band rehearsal as an audience of one.

A further point the results emphasize is that students perceive a lack of respect in their schools. While nearly two thirds of all students said they believe teachers respect them—a worrisome result in and of itself—the fact that far fewer think students respect teachers is very troubling. The gap here between student and teacher perceptions is dramatic, as nearly all teachers say they respect students. If teachers are in a position to inspire and support students through their learning, the challenge of doing so increases significantly if there is an essential lack of respect on either side. Like care, respect correlates highly with indicators that have an impact on student achievement. It is a fact of human nature that we work harder for people we believe respect us and who we respect. In a school setting, that hard work translates into academic achievement.

Regarding respect between teachers and students, while it may seem obvious, it bears stating: In the reciprocal relationship that is respect between a teacher and a student—I respect you if you respect me—the adult has to go first. We have heard teachers say, "I don't give respect until I get respect" or "When kids show me respect, that's when I respect them." We always think they will be waiting a long time. Maybe it's our age, but neither of us at 50-plus is waiting around for some 13-year-olds (we have socks that are older) to respect us before we show them respect.

There is no way to disrespectfully teach someone who is disrespectful to respect you. The only way to *teach* respect, to get another person who is being disrespectful to respect you, is to model respect for them *in spite of* their disrespect for you. It turns out that when someone treats you disrespectfully, if you respect them, they come to learn what real respect is and to *then* treat you with respect. The lesson may both require repetition and take awhile to sink in, but most worthwhile lessons do.

While we may wish there was a universal definition and understanding of respect, it just isn't reality. In some cultures, respect means looking a person in the eye, in other cultures it is disrespectful to do so. When we walk into a school building and hear a teacher or administrator screaming (and we mean screaming) at students in the hallways, our immediate, instinctive reaction is that this behavior from the adult is disrespectful. The administrator, however, often feels she is actually showing respect because she wants students in classrooms and learning. Given these differences, the only solution is to find common ground.

The low level of respect revealed in the survey is not restricted to teacher-student relationships. Perhaps most alarming is that just one in three students believes that students respect one another. Students, too, are in a position to be heroes and role models to their peers. Under these circumstances, the chances of such student-to-student support will be difficult to foster. Beyond that, a respectful environment is better suited to learning. Meaningful classroom discussions, collaboration, asking questions in the class, helping another student who is having difficulty, and admitting to having difficulty are all much easier in a climate of mutual respect. Creating such an environment is an excellent opportunity for educators and students to work together as partners, and is essential to effective teaching and learning.

33% of students agree "Students respect each other." These students are . . .

- 8 times more likely to feel that students are supportive of each other
- 4 times more likely to believe that school is preparing them well for their futures
- 4 times more likely to think that school is a welcoming and friendly place
- 3 times more likely to say they enjoy being at school
- 3 times more likely to indicate that they enjoy participating in their classes

. . . than students who do not agree that students respect each other.

One of the most troubling statistics from the My Voice survey falls in this category of Heroes. Nearly half the students in this country do not think teachers care if they are in school—just 51% of students agree that teachers care if they are absent from school! Before we can expect students to meet their academic potential, educators should at the very least let students know we care whether they are even present. When a student is absent for any length of time, is he or she welcomed back with offers of assistance and support? Or do they get the subtle, or not so subtle, message that their absence and subsequent return is an inconvenience to their teachers?

The Condition of Heroes is powerful. Every day, adults in school have the opportunity to alter the course of a young person's life. We have seen countless times that a caring adult who says hello, who offers a word of encouragement, who asks about an afterschool event, or who inquires about an ailing parent can have an impact far beyond the effort put into those simple gestures of kindness and respect. Students and adults alike have told us stories about the heroes they met in school who continue to have profound influence on them. We believe that, far too often, teachers do not realize that these encounters have a deep and lasting power.

---

CR80

## CONDITION 3: SENSE OF ACCOMPLISHMENT

*You want to be recognized for the work you do because you did it and you're happy about it. You want people to know that it's a proud moment.*

—fifth-grade female student

*I am a lower student and I try really hard with some of my teachers, but whenever I don't do good, they disapprove of me. They like the smarter kids better.*

—seventh-grade male student

Some of the most rewarding and meaningful experiences in life are the ones that require us to work the hardest. We have all enjoyed the true satisfaction of a challenging job well done. The task itself, so long as it is meaningful to us, is somewhat beside the point; training to run a marathon, revising a thesis paper multiple times, or raking a sprawling lawn of autumn leaves can all deliver the sweetness of hard-earned accomplishment. This means we feel pride both in the accomplishment, as well as in the commitment and work we contributed toward its outcome. These experiences show us that determination, passion, and hard work are the real keys to success.

School, and indeed life, can be challenging. Without question, schools should focus on achievement, with the ultimate goal being for students to reach their fullest potential. The key to this success, however, is to pay attention to more than just academic achievement. On the way to academic success, each student's effort, perseverance, and citizenship must be acknowledged and supported. The goal must not simply be for students to achieve, but also for them to learn *how to achieve*. Educators must commit to celebrating the entire learning process rather than focusing solely on its outcomes. We must ask and assess: How did students get to this point? What obstacles did they face and how did they choose to handle them? Likewise, we need to focus on how students treated others along the way: Did their choices reflect awareness, concern, and respect?

# On a Roll

Most schools have assemblies that recognize students for their academic or athletic prowess. Students who get As are fêted with certificates in Honor Roll assemblies. Student athletes get to run through butcher block paper painted with the school's mascot, while the cheerleaders and other students applaud enthusiastically.

One high school started to wonder why their school celebrated such a narrow range of talents and efforts. There were plenty of students who contributed to the school in other positive ways: By helping others above and beyond expectations, by modeling effort regardless of outcomes, by commitment to co-curricular activities besides sports. Students and teachers worked together to expand their Honor Roll assemblies and pep rallies to include an "On a Roll" award and recognition of nonsport co-curricular activity. Students who had been "caught being good," students who had raised Fs or Ds to Cs and Bs, students who had made a positive contribution to their school's drama program or school band, or who had started the Guitar Hero club were celebrated with balloons and applause and a chance to run through the school banner.

The entire school community started to see how richly talented the student body was. School pride increased. "Jocks" gave "geeks" high fives. In general, school morale improved and cliquish behavior diminished—all from seeing "accomplishment" as more than an A in class or a victory on the field.

As students arrive at school each day, they must be welcomed into an environment that acknowledges their effort, celebrates their perseverance, and supports the positive choices they make as citizens of the school community. When students' experiences encompass all of this, they will grow personally, socially, emotionally, and academically. We must be sure to equip students with the ability to reach their fullest potential and make a difference in this world. We have done our jobs as educators when all the young people we teach are able to experience a true Sense of Accomplishment, not only as students, but as citizens of the world. Here is what students have to say about how well we are meeting that charge.

| SENSE OF ACCOMPLISHMENT STATEMENTS | % IN AGREEMENT |
| --- | --- |
| I am encouraged to practice good citizenship at school. | 77% |
| Teachers recognize students who are kind and helpful. | 73% |
| I have never been recognized for something positive at school. | 25% |
| I give up when school work is difficult. | 18% |
| Teachers recognize me when I try my best. | 60% |
| Teachers let my parents know what I do well. | 51% |
| I put forth my best effort at school. | 77% |
| Getting good grades is important to me. | 91% |

The gap between wanting to achieve academically (91% of students) and putting forth the energy and time to achieve academically (77% of students) is concerning. We have talked with students who ascribed getting good grades to luck or teacher favoritism or innate intelligence rather than to effort. The data also reveal that schools need to do a better job of recognizing student accomplishments of all sorts, including celebrating signs of good citizenship. Schools are very good at recognizing intellectual aptitude and certain types of success (e.g., high grades, athletic ability). Yet students need to be recognized by their teachers for the hard work they put in to assignments and for their unique talents and interests. In addition, schools need to develop the rewards and celebrations that promote this type of an environment.

In an intriguing article titled "From Aptitude to Effort: A New Foundation for Our Schools," Resnick argues that we need to move away from the current system that is based on intellectual ability toward one based on effort. She writes that the possibility "that effort actually creates ability, that people can become smart by working hard at the right kinds of learning tasks has never been taken seriously in America or indeed in any European society, although it is the guiding assumption of education institutions in societies with a Confucian tradition" (1995, p. 56). Imagine schools with report cards that kept a record of effort on a par with academic achievement and awards assemblies that praised those who worked hardest as well as those who scored highest.

## Simple Calculus

A high school math teacher shared the following story about one of our classes:

At the time I took the graduate course in Aspirations offered in our district, I was teaching AP calculus. I have to admit I was a fence sitter when it came to the whole Aspirations thing. I was open to it and figured a few easy graduate credits couldn't hurt, but it seemed like most of the ideas fell in the category of "Guidance"—at least in high school. For the course, we had to keep a journal, and the assignment for Sense of Accomplishment was to interview a student who drives us up the wall and back down again, and find out what he had accomplished recently.

I dreaded the assignment because I knew I would have to speak to Ted, a junior in my class who drove me crazy because I knew he was getting a C on raw talent, with little study or effort. I asked him to see me after school, assuring him that he wasn't in trouble. When he showed up, I explained that he was a homework assignment (though I didn't say why), and that I wanted to know what he felt he had accomplished lately.

Ted thought for a minute and with a grin said, "My buddies and I have this garage band. We've been playing together for about two years and had our first gig last weekend. You know Melissa? It was her 16th birthday party. It was a blast. We felt like rock stars. People were saying we should play at the Junior Prom. I suppose that's my most recent accomplishment." I asked Ted what instrument he played, and he said, "Lead guitar." I chuckled and shared that I had been playing acoustic guitar for about 30 years. We wound up having a 30-minute conversation that ranged from the Beatles to guitar models. For the rest of that year, Ted turned in all his homework on time, something he had rarely done before and nearly aced every quiz and test, something he only did when he studied. For 30 minutes of chit-chat about a subject I loved, I got further with this student than I had with my constant harping (no pun intended) about missing assignments and the need for more effort. I hopped off the fence on the side of Aspirations.

Pretty simple calculation: Aspirations made me a better calculus teacher.

Students appear to understand what schools expect of them in terms of academic achievement. Though the percentages could be higher, the majority of students say they understand the significance of testing, and most consider getting good grades important. While the My Voice survey does not help determine *why* good grades are important to students (e.g., to get into college, to stay on a sports team, to win the praise of parents), it does show that students who internalize (as "important to me") the value of good grades have an overall more positive experience of school than do their peers who do not agree that getting good grades is important. "Getting good grades" is a clear, if narrow, expression of the values of the school as a learning institution. While we know the hoped for outcomes of an education are far broader than letters on a report card—so say the mission statements of many schools—report cards remain among the most tangible, and sometimes sole, representation of what "counts" in school. To the extent that students internalize the value of grades, the institution that promotes that value will be a more comfortable place.

## IMPROVING THE ODDS

Most students—though not all—who affirm the value of getting good grades also say they put forth their best effort at school. Those who do not presumably think good grades come about in some other way or do not need to put forth their best effort to get good grades. According to McGlarry Klose writing in *Principal Leadership*: "Concepts of ability and effort are interrelated. Some adolescents believe that ability can be improved by applying more effort, and others believe that ability is a fixed quantity and no amount of effort will change it. A positive motivational orientation includes the belief that one's effort does affect one's outcomes, and a negative motivational orientation is demonstrated by a belief that effort will have little or no effect on achievement outcomes" (Klose, 2008, p. 13).

Students attribute success in school to a variety of factors. They may attribute good grades to internal factors like hard work or external factors like a teacher liking them. Furthermore, the cause of getting a good grade may be stable, for example "being smart," or unstable, for example "working hard" (Dweck, 1986). If students believe that internal, stable causes are the only path to success in school, then effort is irrelevant—you are either smart and get good grades, or you are not. If students attribute success to external causes, whether stable ("This teacher never likes me") or not (luck), they similarly see no point in making any effort. "What is crucial to effective learning is that students attribute both success and failure to internal, unstable causes" (Black, Harrison, Lee, Marshall, & William, 2003, p. 75). Effort and perseverance are internal, unstable causes recognized by Sense of Accomplishment.

Students who agreed with the statement "Getting good grades is important to me" are 15 times more likely to report putting forth their best effort than students who do not value the importance of good grades. In addition, students who desire good grades are seven times more likely to enjoy learning. The grade conscious are also 11 and 12 times more likely to push themselves academically and work hard to reach their goals, respectively, 13 times more likely to set high goals, and 9 times more likely to be excited about the future.

91% of students say that "Getting good grades is important to me." These students are . . .

- 15 times more likely to say they put forth their best effort in school
- 13 times more likely to think it is important to set high goals
- 12 times more likely to believe they work hard to reach their goals
- 11 times more likely to say they push themselves to do better academically
- 9 times more likely to say they are excited about their futures
- 7 times more likely to indicate they enjoy learning new things
- 7 times more likely to feel they learn new things that are interesting to them at school

. . . than students who do not agree that grades are important to them.

Clearly, helping students understand and value the importance of good grades will help them work harder, be engaged more, and set goals that challenge them.

Effort in the present is one thing, perseverance over time is another. The ability to stay with academic challenges, to not give up easily, may be one of the best predictors of long-term success in school as well as in life. "Grit," a similar characteristic, has become a hot topic in education (see Tough, 2012). Note that this is a negatively worded statement to get at perseverance: "I give up when school work is difficult." Thus, our odds must be interpreted differently.[2] The students who agreed or strongly agreed with this statement are nearly four times more likely to find school boring and only half as likely to enjoy participating in their classes as those who did not agree with this statement. As one would expect, these students also push themselves academically and work hard to reach their goals at just one third the rate of their peers. These students also feel less supported by their teachers when they make mistakes.

18% of students admit they "give up when schoolwork is difficult." These students are . . .

- 4 times more likely to think school is boring
- 3 times less likely to say they put forth their best effort at school
- 3 times less likely to say they push themselves to do better academically
- 3 times less likely to believe they work hard to reach their goals
- 2 times less likely to say they enjoy participating in class
- 2 times less likely to say they enjoy learning new things
- 2 times less likely to feel that teachers help them learn from their mistakes

. . . than students who say they do not give up when school work is difficult.

Encouraging effort and perseverance is about the messages about learning we impart to students every day. Do we constantly talk about tests, passing end-of-course assessments, and final grades? While these events are a reality of school and, ultimately, receiving a high school diploma, they need not drive what it means to learn. Teachers who help students pass tests *and* love learning have several common characteristics. In their classrooms, these teachers recognize all types of achievement. For example, in English classes final essays *and* pictorial representations of books *and* readers' reflections are posted. We have worked with teachers who leave an open response on all their tests. The open response simply says, "Share in whatever format you want what you have learned in this unit." These teachers give equal weight to how the student represents her learning. Another strategy we see often in elementary schools is teachers providing students the opportunity to redo work until they are satisfied with their own efforts.

A final aspect of Sense of Accomplishment is recognizing good citizenship. Here we are not talking about participation in student government, or even participation

---

[2]Because this is a negative statement, we must consider the inverse impact of the correlation. Thus, the formula for determining the odds is 1 ÷ the odds ratio. For example, students who agree with the statement "I am afraid to try something if I think I may fail" are 2.04 times (1 ÷ .49) *less* likely to agree with the statement "I feel comfortable asking questions in class."

in large-scale projects like collecting food for the needy during the holidays or other service learning. Those efforts are important and will be studied under the Condition of Leadership & Responsibility. Here we are talking about the little acts of kindness and assistance that should be part of life in a school community—picking up a piece of paper in the hallway, holding the door open for a teacher or student with an armful of books, helping someone who has dropped a cafeteria tray full of food. When students are recognized for these nonacademic, nonathletic, nonartistic acts of citizenship, their self-worth is deepened and they feel more a part of the school community. Kindness, like effort, is an unstable, internal cause of behavior.

Students who agree that teachers recognize students who are kind and helpful are three times more likely to agree that school is a welcoming and accepting place, and four times more likely to take greater pride in their school than students who do not agree that students are recognized for being kind and helpful. These students are also six times more likely to feel cared for by their teachers, as well as eight times more likely to have a sense that teachers enjoy working with students. Students who feel noted for their acts of kindness also experience greater enjoyment in school, encouragement to be creative, relevance, and opportunity to make decisions.

**73% of students believe that "Teachers recognize students who are kind and helpful." These students are . . .**

- 8 times more likely to believe that teachers enjoy working with students
- 6 times more likely to think teachers care about them as individuals
- 5 times more likely to feel teachers encourage students to make decisions
- 4 times more likely to say they are proud of their school
- 4 times more likely to report they are encouraged to be creative at school
- 4 times more likely to believe school is preparing them well for their futures
- 3 times more likely to feel school is a welcoming and friendly place
- 3 times more likely to say they enjoy participating in classes
- 3 times more likely to believe their classes help them understand what is happening in their everyday lives

**. . . than students who do not agree kind and helpful students are recognized.**

Nearly all school mission statements mention at least two goals that everyone is working toward. One is academic achievement; the other is citizenship. Rarely does a student receive a diploma if the school knows he or she is not literate or is unable to do basic levels of math. Many systems of assessment assure teachers and administrators that the school has met the challenge of its academic mission before graduating students. Yet how many students who are nowhere near ready to be contributing members of their communities graduate from high school? One can almost hear the sigh of relief from the principal who graduates a student who can read, write, and do math, but who was trouble to the school (i.e., *not* a citizen of the school) until the very end. When a school withholds a diploma from a student who has not proven himself or herself to be a contributing member of the school as readily as it withholds one from a student who cannot add, then we will know that school takes its mission to foster citizenship seriously.

## UNINTENDED MISSTEPS AND INTENTIONAL NEXT STEPS

Looking back over the three Conditions that promote Self-Worth—Belonging, Heroes, and Sense of Accomplishment—not all of our observations in schools represent the best of these conditions. We rarely meet educators who intentionally try to alienate students, put themselves forward as negative role models, or discourage effort. We do, however, see many practices and procedures that make promoting Self-Worth challenging. Some of these, sadly, are common. For example, in some schools the hallways are empty—void of colors, mottos, and any visual appeal. Students and adults want to enter a space that feels and looks welcoming and that inspires pride, yet most schools feel sterile, uninviting, and institutional. Work together with students and maintenance personnel to paint, decorate, and furnish learning spaces that are welcoming and warm.

Another common Belonging misstep occurs when students' schedules change multiple times during the first month of school. Presumably this is sometimes beyond control, yet every effort should be made to avoid this disruptive shuffle that makes a kind of first impression on students who feel less like people and more like parts of a puzzle that someone is trying to fit together. Those responsible for scheduling should do everything possible to ensure a smooth and steady opening of the year. While not all eventualities can be foreseen, the impact on students' sense of self should be considered alongside logistical concerns such as class size and schedule.

Most educators we know are in the profession precisely because they are Heroes. Yet school schedules that allow little breathing space or down time make it nearly impossible for teachers and students to get to know each other as people. The insistence that teachers teach "bell to bell" has a similar effect. Limitations on teachers and students interacting on social media are well intentioned and, obviously, student safety is paramount. Yet as students increasingly use social media to interact, overly restrictive policies on Internet use leave the adults who could and should assert a positive influence seeming out of touch. Discussing professional, yet personable, ways of interacting with students should be part of staff meetings and staff development. New teachers in particular could benefit from hearing the boundary concerns of more experienced staff and veteran teachers could learn from younger staff how to create social media accounts that do not blur the lines between the personal and the private.

Another common practice in schools with unintended consequences is the way adults address each other in a building. Commonly we hear teachers and administrators address each other by their last names: Mrs. Inman, Mr. Connelly, Ms. Hellerstein, yet custodians, bus drivers, and lunch workers are referred to as Sue, Brian, and Julie. This sends the implicit message to students within earshot that there is a social hierarchy, that some adults are more deserving of respect than others. No one intends this as disrespectful, and yet most would agree that a better practice would be to address all adults in a similar manner.

Unintended consequences of the traditional report card are among the greatest deterrents to Sense of Accomplishment. When only the end product is valued, the effort to obtain that end product goes unrecognized. In the confidentiality promised in focus groups, students confess to a range of methods for obtaining good grades on report cards, from cramming to cheating. High-stakes testing is taking a similar toll on schools. The drive to produce a score diminishes learning for learning's sake. We cannot begin to count the number of schools that implicitly reinforce this message late in the school year. When standardized testing is over and several weeks of school remain, the number of field trips, field days, and "fun" activities rises. Rather than spreading these appropriately throughout the year as learning experiences and opportunities to build relationships, schools send the implied message that, absent the test, the effort to continue learning is unnecessary.

Improving students' experiences of Belonging, Heroes, and Sense of Accomplishment, and so Self-Worth, is as much a matter of removing or renovating aspects of the inherited model of school as it is adding or creating wholly new experiences for students.

CHAPTER 5

# Students Speak About Engagement

*More teachers should show that they enjoy what they are doing, because if they are into it, we are too. If they don't, it's impossible to listen, because it's too boring.*

—eighth-grade female student

*When my teachers challenge me to do stuff that is more challenging, they push me because they know I am able. They have confidence in me as a learner, and they help me when I do not understand . . . building my confidence and a mutual respect.*

—twelfth-grade male student

There is little question that Self-Worth is foundational for students to achieve in school and build high aspirations. Students who value themselves and their abilities are likely to both take more away from and contribute more to their school community than those who do not. When students feel accepted for who they are, when they have adults and peers they respect and can turn to as needed, and when they are recognized for their efforts as well as their outcomes, they develop the capacity to excel in school and life. Believing in one's self is necessary if one is to aspire and succeed, yet it is not enough. The goal of improving the educational system is not to create self-assured, ignorant graduates. If students are to *achieve* their aspirations and not just dream about them, they must be actively engaged in the learning process.

Student engagement has come under much scrutiny in the last several years. There is overlap, but little agreement, in the research and literature on the subject (Fredricks, Blumenfeld, & Paris, 2004). Student engagement comprises three broad categories—affective, cognitive, and behavioral—with no single dimension sufficing fully to engage students (Yonezawa & Jones, 2009). A multidimensional approach employs all three Conditions we have identified with the Guiding Principle of Engagement:

- Fun & Excitement relates to students' emotional investment in what they are learning;

- Curiosity & Creativity is connected to students' intellectual engagement with what they are learning; and

- Spirit of Adventure reflects students' willingness to engage in the behaviors (at times risky) necessary to learn.

Despite countless reform efforts, educators still seem at a loss for how to engage today's students. Citing several research studies, an article in the *Journal for Educational Change* posits: "The dilemma . . . is that the field [of education] and the myriad of reforms over the last decade have simultaneously made few inroads to ensure that the quality of curriculum and pedagogical practices are pertinent to young people. Higher behavioral engagement increases students' expectations of success. But American high schools retain a traditional core curriculum that addresses classic content through traditional pedagogical practices" (Yonezawa, Jones, & Joselowsky, 2009, p. 193). In other words, the inherited model of school simply does not work for today's students.

There has been an important shift in our world that has impacted the very nature of the learning, if not the teaching, dynamic. That shift has yet to make its way into many classrooms and schools in a way that is relevant to students and impacts their engagement. Before widespread use of personal computers and the Internet, acquiring information was much more challenging. Many facts and figures could be found only in libraries, textbooks, and the heads of experts. If one wanted or needed to be an educated person (and not everyone did), one needed information. Schools were places where information was stored, dispensed, interpreted, and judged. The interpretive context was a common and agreed upon set of cultural understandings—for the most part Western, white, and male. In addition to dispensing information, schools were expected to socialize students into this worldview.

■ ■ ■ ASSESS YOUR STARTING POINT

Use the best practices for fostering student engagement below to rate yourself on a scale of 0-10, where 0 is never and 10 is always.

- My students are actively involved in their learning.

- My classroom is a dynamic teaching and learning environment.

- My lessons are relevant to students' everyday lives.

- I understand the unique learning styles of all my students.

- I know what piques the curiosity of my students.

- I value and celebrate creative thinking.

- My classes are challenging.

- Students want to be successful in my class. ∎

Teachers went to universities to master subject matter and develop pedagogical skills so that they could mediate between the academic experts and students in developmentally appropriate ways. Many of our schools and classrooms were designed when this was the prevailing paradigm in education. The school "master" stood in front of the classroom to impart information to novices sitting more or less attentively in neat rows. Student "engagement," for the most part, meant students paying attention to the teacher, taking notes, doing their homework, and studying for tests and exams. This was an ideal system for a society trying to produce high school graduates who were a literate and competent industrial work force and citizenry. Those of modest or struggling academic ability obtained jobs. The more academically successful in such a system continued their schooling into college and advanced degrees and entered careers and professions as managers and leaders, doctors and lawyers. Those most attuned to academic life went back to the educational system itself as teachers and administrators at all levels in order to ensure its ongoing functioning. This system of education was successful in its time.

## REFLECT ON YOUR SURROUNDINGS

- What has changed most significantly regarding students' levels of interest and participation since you were the age of your students?

- How do you create interdisciplinary lessons with colleagues to better engage students?

- How do you assess students' levels of interest in your class and their participation in school as a whole?

- What do you do to understand and appreciate your students' learning styles and different intelligences?

- How do you create opportunities for students to be creative in your class?

- How would your students describe an engaging lesson?

- What online resources are available to augment student learning in your subject?

*(Continued)*

Today, however, we face a far different challenge. Now information is everywhere. Schools are not the only places students can get information, and the worldwide nature of information makes the one-stop shop that is the traditional school seem quaint. For example, it makes little sense to most "digital natives" (those who grow up with digital technology) to store information in their heads. Ask any 12-year-old a question she does not know the answer to and, assuming she is near a computer, she can have an answer for you in under one minute. If she is clever, she will even know how reliable the information is. Given that nearly everyone has a cell phone and every cell phone has a camera, everyone has, literally, a photographic memory. What everyone may *not* be able to do is understand the information or be able to see the value or relevance in it or how to apply it. The educational problem is no longer that information is difficult to come by; on the contrary, the current problem is that information is too easy to come by.

# Environmentalism

To note, I am far from an environmentalist. I drive a Jeep, own a fishing boat, and am Platinum on several airlines. My carbon footprint is a size 14. Nonetheless, at every turn during my travels, I am more and more enamored by the beauty that occurs naturally: the changing colors of leaves in fall, a moonlit snow fall in winter, the water gushing down mountains in spring, and the rosy sunsets of summer. Sheer beauty, inspiring all on its own, that neither we nor Disney had to create or charge an admission fee to see.

How does this relate to education and engagement? Unfortunately, very little. In the current landscape of education, almost everything seems to be manmade, structured, (overly) designed, planned, calculated, deliberated, assessed, tested, and ranked. There is very little that is truly "natural," and quite frankly, that is more than a bit depressing. Our schools have the most beautiful natural resource in the world—students—and in so many ways, we fail to recognize, appreciate, and foster this beauty.

Each student has a unique personality, indeed an inner beauty, with individual hopes and dreams. However, students are placed into a school environment that has a prescribed aesthetic, that strips kids of their personalities, replaces them with conformity and normativeness, and somewhat dictates their hopes and dreams—in some ways, restricting both nature and beauty.

If we had a "class" for trees, we would make sure they all had the same number of branches and turned the exact same color on the same day each year. If the Grand Canyon were a student, schools would try to assess its beauty with a tape measure. If schools were in charge of waterfalls, they would only run during certain times of the day and at a prescribed rate (pacing guides, anyone?). As currently run, schools are blind to the full beauty of the students. We have become educational anti-environmentalists!

What would happen if we had just a little less proscribed pedagogy and a bit more guidance, coaching, and encouragement? When driven by an environment that encourages spontaneity and recognizes the natural beauty of students, schools can be stunning places. Regardless of your perspective—be it a multivehicle carbon scarfer or a crunchy granola naturalist—the lesson is clear: Schools should focus a lot less on scaffolding, structuring, and assessing the learning, and a great deal more on discovering and encouraging the unique beauty within each and every student.

*—RJQ*

Even the social reasons for going to school are seemingly less relevant than they were in the past. We live in an age when a young person can "chat" with his friends without ever leaving the house or picking up a telephone. One of the more common discipline concerns we hear in schools is texting during class—students texting friends they will see in one hour in the cafeteria! We adults just don't get it. Add gaming into this mix and it gets more and more challenging for the reality that is school to compete with a virtual universe that is nearly infinite in scope. Students inhabit a world where they can "participate" in the Battle for Anzio instead of reading about it, where they can be "published" authors with no regard for grammar or spelling instead of being quizzed on grammar and spelling, where they can be friends with someone in France instead of completing a unit in a French workbook about friends, and where they can create YouTube videos with the "viral" potential to be seen by thousands of people instead of watching a DVD in a darkened classroom. In all honesty, how far beyond the film strips of 40 years ago are most efforts at PowerPoint?

Engagement, therefore, must begin by accepting that this is the wide webbed world of our students and that, like it or not, the expert-novice tables have tilted, if not turned. Schools and teachers are doing their best to keep up technologically, but engagement is not simply about technology. Students tell us that having interactive whiteboards in the classroom is great but gets boring quickly if only the teacher gets to use them. They like having PowerPoint as an option for presenting projects but are frustrated by the firewall that won't let them access the music they want to add as a soundtrack. They are grateful for the new computer lab but don't understand why they can't listen to an MP3 player while using a design program. And they think it's simply dumb that their school bans smartphone use.

##  COMMIT TO A DIRECTION

- Create open-ended assignments that allow for creativity.
- Use portfolios to measure success as well as mastery.
- Incorporate art, music, physical movement, and digital technology into teaching.
- Connect lessons to local, national, and global current events.

- Limit worksheets and lectures.
- Ensure that the class is rigorous for all students.
- Develop a safe learning environment where students are not afraid of success.
- Require students to develop and monitor personal, social, and academic goals. ■

The easy availability of information and high-tech wizardry of the new millennium suggest three consequences for engagement of our students. First, educators need to face the finding that nearly half of all students (44%) say they are bored in school (QISA, 2013). Schools must help students learn to connect to information with interest, passion, and emotion. For all their ability to enhance communication, e-mailing, text messaging, chatting, blogging, and so on are emotionless. Smilies and other emoticons are a poor substitute for discovering a genuine emotional connection to what one is reading and viewing. Is it a coincidence that an interest in Emotional Intelligence has coincided with the rise of digital communication? Fun & Excitement is less about teachers entering into an unwinnable competition with Pixar and Nintendo and more about providing an education that accounts for the heart as a guide to all that the head has access to. When the whole student is involved in learning—head, heart, and hands—students become so engaged in what they are doing that they lose track of space and time. This full spectrum approach to reality is the best counterbalance to the lure of the virtual.

Second, schools must also foster the use of imagination when interacting with information. Students are naturally curious and creative; however, these inclinations too often fade over time. Many argue that for all their fireworks, modern technology dulls the imagination of young people by doing all their imagining for them. At the same time, many prominent educational writers bemoan the fact that our current approach to schooling dissipates, if not downright discourages, students' curiosity and creativity (Bronson & Merryman, 2010; Kim, 2011). In sixth grade, 78% of students agree with the statement: "At school I am encouraged to be creative." In twelfth grade just 62% of students agree.

This is not just about tight budgets that lead districts to cut art classes (though that does not help). Rather, it is about taking a whole new approach to education—one in which the principle goal is to develop an *imaginative and flexible mind*, rather than one that is filled with fixed content, and one that helps students think divergently and see multiple answers, rather than learn how to converge on a single right answer from four choices. The tardiness of this shift led Bill Gates to say in 2005 that our current school system is "obsolete" (Gates, 2005). Students must be encouraged and taught to ask "Why?" and "Why not?" We must teach students how to ask relevant questions and how to apply what they learn in meaningful and creative ways. If we are asking our students questions they can look up on the Internet, we are asking the wrong questions.

## OVERCOME OBSTACLES

**Standards, pacing guides, and mandates leave no time for creativity.** Building creativity into the curriculum needs to be purposeful. Unfortunately, with increased pressure on testing and meeting standards, we lose sight of the fact that meaningful learning and engagement requires imagination from both the teacher and student. Free your mind of rules and regulations and you will be surprised how creative you and your students become—and, in turn, meet and surpass standards.

**I am not an entertainer and my students are used to being entertained.** There is a difference between entertaining and engaging. An entertaining teacher is the center of attention, whereas a teacher who engages students provides tools and resources in order for them to be the attentive center of their learning.

**You can't measure creativity.** The thought that you can't measure creativity displays how trapped we are by our own thinking. Creativity

*(Continued)*

(Continued)

manifests itself through originality and usefulness. Creativity indeed cannot and should not be measured using conventional standards. Rather, consider each student's progress in his or her ability to represent ideas in original and valuable ways. Are students able to represent historical ideas in a way that is not simply paraphrasing something they read online? Are students able to "see" new ways of representing math concepts developed by Euclid more than 2,000 years ago? Can students use multimedia to represent a concept that is traditionally seen only through words?

**My students are satisfied with just barely passing my class.** Herein lies the problem. If the goal of learning is simply to pass a class, then for many students just barely passing is still passing. However, if the goal of learning is for students to be emotionally, intellectually, and behaviorally engaged, then it would be a challenge to find any student, or adult for that matter, who just wanted to be barely engaged.

**Students are driven by grades and end product, not the learning process.** When students enter preschool, they have no notion of grades—only their parents do! The learning process is natural, exciting, and what school is all about. Think of all a young child learns, including speaking a language fluently, before entering school without ever once getting a grade. Learning is a self-correcting process that needs little in the way of external carrots or sticks. We can't blame students for being driven by grades when many adults only emphasize grades. Let your students know that learning is about growth and exploration and reward them accordingly. ■

Third, in order to promote Engagement, schools and teachers need to encourage healthy risk taking. On the one hand, attaining information is too easy. On the other hand, the overwhelming volume of information and the dizzying array of choices available to today's young people can cause paralysis. In addition, high-stakes testing has diminished risk taking in students. One third of students (32%) say they are afraid to try something if they think they will fail (QISA, 2013). We also have heard from students that they are afraid to succeed. Doing well in school can create Belonging problems for some students. Educators wishing to help students dream about the future, and inspire them in the present to reach those dreams, need to find ways to avoid both complacency and consternation in their students. Developing a Spirit of Adventure toward one's goals and the effort needed to attain them is something schools should be cultivating in their students.

# ARRIVE

In schools that develop Engagement in students:

- Students know what they are learning is relevant to their lives.
- Students are self-directed learners.
- Teachers' lessons are always evolving and changing depending on the students and current events.

- Teachers are passionate about teaching and their subject matter.
- The school board requires more than letter grades on report cards.
- Administrators solicit new ideas and opinions from staff and students.
- Community supports the arts, technology, and creativity opportunities as much as athletics. ■

While efforts to close the achievement gap are noble, we must question how much farther we will get without first closing the participation gap. This can only be done by helping students become meaningfully engaged in their classes and in the life of the school. Students who are not achieving do not fall short because of an innate absence of passion, a deficit of curiosity or creativity, or a lack of desire to take risks. Many are not achieving because school is not connecting to their interests, imaginations, or impulse to take a chance. In short, far too many students are checked out. Many go to school because they are required to, do just enough to get by (or else get out as soon as they can), and wind up in college or work ill-prepared for the next level. Recent efforts by many states to raise the dropout age to 18, while well intentioned, will not solve the underlying problem of disengagement—which for many is a cause of dropping out as well as a host of other negative behaviors (Henry, Knight, & Thornberry, 2012). You can't make a bad meatloaf better by cooking it longer. Even many who are successful in school are not full and active participants. Rather, they have found out how to interact with a system that asks little more of them than to get good grades by being the attentive, but passive, spectators of the work of well-meaning adults. We can and must do better.

*I like when we do projects, have fun, but still learn.*

—fifth-grade female student

*If I could change anything about the school, I would do less lectures. I can't just sit and listen all day.*

—eleventh-grade male student

Fun . . . an often forbidden F-word in education. Why is it so frightening? In life, we embrace fun activities. Time flies when we are engaged and happy. We appreciate spending time with upbeat and enthusiastic people. Why should it be any different in the classroom?

It's as if someone declared that if you're having fun, you can't be learning . . . that the muscles that control the smile simultaneously block knowledge from entering our brains. While it may not be cited in teacher resource books, we have known a lot of teachers who believed this was true. We even had an elementary school principal once argue against Fun & Excitement as a condition in schools, saying that schools had a duty to bore students at times in order to teach them that life is not always fun. We feel quite safe saying this is not true and in fact proclaim just the opposite: More learning occurs when students are having fun, and better teaching occurs when teachers are having fun, too.

When we mention this philosophy to educators, we sometimes hear, "But I'm not an entertainer!" Make no mistake, "fun" should not be understood to mean students running wild or rolling around on the floor laughing at jokes. We are not suggesting that teachers should become stand-up comedians. However, teachers are, in part, engagers, as they are charged with capturing the attention of an audience. Fun in school means engaging the learning process at an emotional level.

## What's On the Menu?

As we visit and work in schools around the world, we have amazing opportunities to meet dynamic and engaging teachers. Among them, we consistently meet culinary arts teachers who simply exude passion. Their love of the business is absolutely contagious. In one culinary class, we listened as the teacher explained the students' assignment for the week: they were to create a new dinner menu. The freedom associated with the assignment created a buzz and excitement.

However, the next set of directions illustrated the teacher's true passion. First, he shared statistics about their community. The statistics included the numbers of families on food stamps, the number of kids who go hungry every day, and the addresses of local food kitchens. Student attention piqued. Then the culinary teacher related that he volunteered as a cook at a local soup kitchen. He described how rewarding this work was for him and that he saw it as an opportunity to use his skills to benefit people who were less fortunate. Finally, he challenged his students to work with a local food pantry or soup kitchen to develop a new and tasty dinner based on the available food at the pantry.

Students were clearly engaged in the challenge. They had a real test at hand, one, related to their interests, and the opportunity to make a difference. This teacher had succeeded in making learning fun, exciting, and altruistic by connecting to students' passions—as well as their emotions.

The phrase "live, learn, laugh," isn't practiced enough in schools. Students can enjoy life and learning, and at the same time be very serious about their academic goals. It sounds paradoxical, but we know it is true that a person can have fun and be serious at the same time. Take, for instance, a sport fisherman. When he goes fishing, he may have fun, but at the same time be determined to catch fish. We know golfers who are serious about improving their game but still have fun doing it. Consider an actor enraged on a stage, causing an audience to cringe in fear, all in good fun. Fun is more than having a good laugh—it's about enthusiastically meeting challenges with focused passion.

Part of a teacher's job is to instill fun in learning. Just put yourself in your students' shoes—would you rather participate in fun and engaging activities or lessons that don't capture your interest? School should be a place students look forward to going, where they are inspired to learn and where they are actively engaged and emotionally involved in their schoolwork. As a result, these students will become more self-confident, passionate, prepared—no, *willing*—to meet the challenges of each school day. To foster this condition in schools, students need to be offered new opportunities, as well as meaningful challenges, that are connected with their unique interests. So, how are we doing?

| FUN & EXCITEMENT STATEMENTS | % IN AGREEMENT |
| --- | --- |
| I enjoy being at school. | 54% |
| Teachers enjoy working with students. | 64% |
| Teachers make school an exciting place to learn. | 42% |
| School is boring. | 44% |
| I enjoy participating in my classes. | 66% |
| Teachers have fun at school. | 47% |
| Learning can be fun. | 73% |

Fun & Excitement is first and foremost about students being emotionally engaged in their learning. To be engaged in learning, students must find it enjoyable and worthwhile. Disengagement is a serious obstacle to learning. In a sense, boredom represents a profound disconnect between the goals of the teacher—which hopefully include not just that he is teaching, but also that his students are learning—and the goal of the learner to be involved in an activity that is interesting or relevant.

What is actually at stake when students are bored is something far deeper than the ho-hum of a lesson—it is a lack of efficacy and autonomy that is itself disengaging. As Fried puts it, "It's easy to say that teachers and students need to communicate better about the reasons behind the activity and how it relates to some goal that the student understands is worth achieving. But that assumes that it is the student's right to be consulted about the purpose of a particular activity or assignment, and there are many teachers and parents who believe that young people have no such inherent right" (2001a, p. 67). Sadly, we have met such teachers and parents and administrators. And gratefully we have met their opposites. What Fried implies is behind the issue of boredom is the issue of whether teachers and students are full partners in what takes place in the classroom and school. That concern is at the very heart of this book—that students must have a meaningful voice in what takes place while they are in school. When students are given a voice, boredom decreases and engagement increases. Students who believe they have a voice in school are seven times more likely to be academically motivated than students who do not believe they have a voice in school (QISA, 2013).

## IMPROVING THE ODDS

The most positive finding from the My Voice survey in this Condition is the nearly three quarters of students who believe learning can be fun. Though this figure could certainly be higher, when contrasted with the high number of students who are bored in school, and the low number who enjoy their classes, we gain insight into what we refer to as "the participation gap." Students who agree that learning can be fun are only one fourth as likely to report that school is boring as those who do not agree that learning can be fun. As one would expect, the numbers are reversed for "I enjoy participating in my classes," with those who believe learning can be fun being six times more likely to enjoy participating in their classes. Other obvious high correlations exist with "I enjoy learning new things" and "I learn new things that are interesting to me at school."

73% of students believe "Learning can be fun." These students are . . .

- 9 times more likely to say they enjoy learning new things
- 8 times more likely to report that they learn new things that are interesting to them at school

- 6 times more likely to say they enjoy participating in their classes
- 4 times less likely to think school is boring

The disparity between the finding that students believe learning can be fun (and so are less likely to be bored in school and more likely to participate in their classes), and the fact that many others do not experience engagement in their school, must be addressed. Students are clearly the potential here, not the problem. Schools must explore more effective ways of tapping into student voice in order to engage them in learning. This is never more clear than when we speak with dropouts. When asked why they dropped out of school, we have heard on too many occasions that "School is boring" and that "There was nothing there for me."

The reason for improving participation by connecting schoolwork with what students find enjoyable and interesting may seem obvious but is worth supporting with the data. Students who enjoy being at school and participating in their classes are more likely to put forth effort and to push themselves to do better academically than students who do not enjoy being at school. They are also more likely to see a greater relevance in what they are doing in the present and for their future. This relevance is then, reciprocally, critical to their engagement. We will continue to struggle in our efforts to close the achievement gap until we address this underlying issue of the participation gap.

54% of students say they "enjoy being at school." These students are . . .

- 4 times more likely to say they put forth their best effort at school
- 4 times more likely to believe they push themselves to do better academically
- 4 times more likely to believe that school is preparing them well for their futures
- 3 times more likely to feel their classes help them understand what is happening in their everyday lives

. . . than students who did not say they enjoyed being at school.

66% of students say they "enjoy participating in classes." These students are . . .

- 5 times more likely to say they put forth their best effort at school
- 5 times more likely to believe that what they learn in school will benefit their futures
- 5 times more likely to believe they push themselves to do better academically

- 4 times more likely to feel their classes help them understand what is happening in their everyday lives

*. . . than students who do not say they enjoy participating in their classes.*

In addition to student boredom, there is the issue of how students perceive their teachers' participation and emotional investment in what is happening in the classroom. The My Voice Survey reveals that students do not experience teachers as especially engaged in the teaching-learning process. Whether this perception is accurate or not, these percentages should be an area of professional concern for all educators. When students can sense their teachers' excitement, their experience of school is much more positive. Students who agree that teachers make school an exciting place to learn are much more likely to perceive care, modeling, accessibility, respect, recognition, enjoyment, creativity, relevance, and assistance in their teachers.

*42% of students agree "Teachers make school an exciting place to learn." These students are . . .*

- 7 times more likely to think teachers respect students
- 7 times more likely to say they enjoy participating in class
- 7 times more likely to feel they are encouraged to be creative at school
- 7 times more likely to say teachers help them learn from their mistakes
- 6 times more likely to think teachers care about them as individuals
- 5 times more likely to feel they have a teacher who is a positive role model for them
- 4 times more likely to believe they have a teacher with whom they can talk if they have a problem

*. . . than students who do not agree that teachers make school an exciting place to learn.*

In *The Passionate Teacher,* Fried writes, "Passionate teaching can only be recognized, ultimately, in terms of students engaging in productive learning that connects with real-world problems and events" (2001b, p. 45). Such an approach, for many teachers and schools, may imply a profound re-orientation of the nature of schooling:

- from something that teachers do *to,* or *for* students, to something that teachers do *with* students,
- from something based mainly in textbooks chosen by teachers, to something based mainly in events in the world of the students,

- from something directed by the experts who write curriculum, to something directed by the interests of the learners,

- from instruction restricted to departmental (and compartmental) learning, to instruction unrestricted by any one discipline at a time, and

- from something that happens mostly inside the school building, to something that happens mostly outside the school building.

## Up or Down?

The Fun & Excitement numbers in one of the U.K. schools we were working with was a cause for alarm for many teachers. In truth, the numbers did not tell them anything they didn't already know: Their students were bored.

After checking in with students in focus groups, a committee of willing teachers from each department spent a year developing a homegrown, project-based curriculum that was interdisciplinary and directly related to the interests of their students. They piloted this in the seventh grade by creating a block period that started each day. Their goal was to improve their Fun & Excitement results on the survey by at least 10 percentage points per indicator.

The course relied heavily on both the World Wide Web and the wide world right outside their door. For example, one unit involved visits to a nearby dried-up riverbed. These daily 90-minute excursions lasted more than two weeks and included geology, anthropology, art, local history, biology, physics, mathematics, poetry, and descriptive writing. A local author and a local conservationist were invited guest instructors. By coincidence, midway through the unit, there was a town meeting to discuss the sale to a developer of the property they had been studying and attendance was assigned as optional. Nearly every student went. The teacher adjusted the next day's classroom lesson from the planned math lesson making use of temperature variations they had collected to a social studies lesson on democracy in town governments.

Guess what happened when they gave the My Voice survey that year? Their Fun & Excitement numbers went *down!* Specifically in the seventh grade!! Some indicators by 15% or more. The teachers involved in creating the curriculum were devastated. We surmised: You made these numbers go down. You made one class out of five off the wall engaging. You started students off in that class every day and then they rolled into their traditional classes. By comparison, you made the rest of the school day seem really dull. Now you have a choice: You can make the rest of the day look like first period or make first period go back to looking like the rest of the day.

We conduct an exercise in our workshops on Fun & Excitement that asks participants to list activities they find generally interesting and engaging. Most lists include being outdoors, with others, and involve physical activity (hiking), or personal involvement (doing a crossword) of some sort. We then ask participants to make a list of activities they generally find boring. Most of these lists include indoor activities done alone that typically involve mindless repetition (e.g., ironing, standing in line, filling out paperwork). We then ask which list looks more like what we ask students to do every day in school (yes, it's a bit of a "gotcha"). Many schools we visit have sorted out how to have students working in groups rather than alone (though schools are still sorting out assessment under those circumstances). Yet many still use outside activities as a reward for good behavior inside, rather than as a lab for all kinds of learning. And physical movement is fairly restricted even though movement and hands-on activities can be engaging and educational. These are no doubt challenging transitions for a school to make, but critically important ones when it comes to student engagement.

Teachers who establish an environment with Fun & Excitement in mind have three things in common:

- Excitement. Their personal enthusiasm is contagious. They make a conscious decision to exude passion even when the subject or lesson may not be dynamic in itself.

- Variety. They vary presentation within a class and no lecture lasts more than 10 minutes.

- Teaming. They frequently team teach with students as partners.

On the student side, there are also several commonalities that make for effectively engaged learning, including the following:

- Collaboration. Students are given myriad ways to participate in a given class period. This may include small group work, partner work, one-on-one work with the teacher, whole-class discussion, interactive computer work, and so on. Whatever the approach, students learn the same concept in more than one way.

- Problem-solving. Discussion and dialogue intentionally stir up controversy. Particularly in a classroom with adolescents, passionate debate and seeing multiple viewpoints, even if no resolution is reached, can be highly engaging. Absent alternative views, teachers become adept at playing devil's advocate.

- Application. Previous days' learning is reinforced through games and applied knowledge. Review is always in a different, and frequently even more engaging, mode than the material was originally presented.

- Relevance. Learners are challenged to connect learning in one class to another. For example, if the history class is learning about the Industrial Revolution, the English class is reading Upton Sinclair and the science class is examining scientific advancements of that era. As learners, students who experience these connections tend to be more engaged in their learning.

The condition of Fun & Excitement in today's schools is not about students laughing and joking instead of studying and learning. It is about students becoming so engaged in what they are learning that they stop watching the clock, checking their phones, or looking out the window. For educators, it is about being so excited about teaching that the passion they have for their subject matter becomes contagious. For all of us, it is about enjoying what we do each and every day. Life is simply way too short to not be happy—both in school and out.

---

∽CℜℵↃ∽

---

## CONDITION 5: CURIOSITY & CREATIVITY

*I like science because you get to do activities; I'm really interested in the solar system.*

—fifth-grade male student

*I'd like more opportunities for creativity, where they give you an idea then you can do your own variation using your own creativity, your own ideas. And change the classroom so it is more alive looking. Having just walls and desks make me so tired; pictures and posters make it more stimulating.*

—tenth-grade male student

If you've ever met a 3-year-old, you know that the desire to learn more about the world around us is indeed innate and is most simply expressed in the questions "Why?" "What?" and "How?" Often referred to as Curiosity, this Condition is closely partnered with Creativity—the Condition that inspires the same 3-year-olds to mix and match socks or try a tutu for a stylish headdress. Creativity is expressed with the questions "Why not?" "What if?" and "How else?"

While Engagement at the emotional level looks like Fun & Excitement, at the cognitive level Engagement is exhibited through Curiosity & Creativity. The Condition of Curiosity & Creativity is characterized by inquisitiveness, eagerness, a strong desire to learn new or interesting things, and a longing to satisfy the mind with new discoveries. These two terms appear together as a single condition because they are both products of an engaged imagination.

The Condition of Curiosity & Creativity encourages students to make full use of their imaginations in order to experience the "high" of exploring and developing new ideas. Currently, there is a trend in education that highlights the importance of fostering creativity in schools. Craft writes, "Creativity has become viewed, since the late 1990s, as centrally relevant to education globally in a way it has perhaps never been before" (2005, p. 3). Similarly, developing Curiosity is seen as critical to education at all levels and across all disciplines (Arnone, 2003).

## CSI HS

If you walk into Mr. O'Brien's science classroom in the spring, there is no telling what madness and mayhem you might meet. An ominous and suspicious looking rabbit sits on the chest of a "dead" crash-test dummy lying in a pool of bright red theatrical blood. The interior of a minivan strewn with a variety of animal hairs and beer bottles. A pane of glass with what looks like two bullet holes. Mr. O'Brien teaches a forensics science course. Students collect dust and evidence using a specially rigged vacuum cleaner. They run each other's fingerprints through a real AFIS (Automatic Fingerprint Identification System) and pluck hair from each other's heads. They use physics to conduct blood spatter analyses and sift through trashcans. They try to match teeth and tread marks to dental records and tire patterns.

Capitalizing on the popularity of the CSI television franchise, as well as on the morbid curiosity of high school juniors and seniors, Mr. O'Brien's class is a tour de force in Fun & Excitement and Curiosity & Creativity. Students are fully engaged from the moment they discover a crime to the day they give "expert" testimony in the courtroom. All the while they are learning science and, more importantly, how to have a scientific mind.

The purpose of the class is to teach the discipline of forensics and at the same time instill the skills necessary to be a thorough and careful observer and thinker. Mr. O'Brien teaches this course not just to nurture future crime scene investigators but also to foster inquisitiveness and ingenuity in all his students.

Despite this trend, the Condition of Curiosity & Creativity is greatly challenged by an educational system obsessed with evaluation and accountability. We want students to be curious, yet we educate them in an environment driven by getting the right answers on a test, rather than learning to ask the right questions that will lead to creative solutions. We want students to be uniquely creative, yet we educate them using common standards and common assessment. Yet, being concretely creative is, by definition, precisely not being common or standard. We should have *creative* curricula, *creative* standards, and *creative* assessment instead of the "common" version of each. Don't we want students to have creative, rather than common, minds?

There is no doubt that the intensity of Curiosity & Creativity tends to diminish over time due to the habituating effects of the environment, and some would say, the process of maturation itself (Schmitt & Lahroodi, 2008, p. 144). Therefore, to sustain student intellectual engagement, schools must work to develop learning environments that invite active questioning and creative exploration and "to preserve the most remarkable features of the young mind—its adventurousness, its generativity, its resourcefulness, and its flashes of flexibility and creativity" (Gardner, 1993, p. 111). What do students think about Curiosity & Creativity in their schools?

| CURIOSITY & CREATIVITY STATEMENTS | % IN AGREEMENT |
|---|---|
| I feel comfortable asking questions in class. | 64% |
| My teachers present lessons in different ways. | 76% |
| At school I am encouraged to be creative. | 67% |
| I enjoy working on projects with other students. | 70% |
| My classes help me understand what is happening in my everyday life. | 44% |
| School inspires me to learn. | 65% |
| I enjoy learning new things. | 80% |
| I learn new things that are interesting to me at school. | 72% |
| What I learn in school will benefit my future. | 79% |

## IMPROVING THE ODDS

To note that 4 out of 5 students like to learn new things is heartening. Students who enjoy learning new things are more likely to put forth their best effort, affirm the importance of good grades, push themselves academically, work hard to reach their goals, and be excited about their future than their disinterested peers. Furthermore, students who are innately curious are nine times more likely to say that school meets their interest in learning new things. Clearly students' natural curiosity must be mined for its potential to be highly self-motivating.

80% of students say "I enjoy learning new things." These students are . . .

- 9 times more likely to think they learn new things that are interesting at school

- 7 times more likely to report that getting good grades is important to them

- 7 times more likely to feel they work hard to reach their goals

- 5 times more likely to say they are excited about their futures
- 5 times more likely to say they put forth their best effort at school
- 5 times more likely to say they push themselves to do better academically
- 4 times more likely to believe they can make a difference in this world

. . . than students who do not agree that they enjoy learning new things.

When schools provide students with educational opportunities that are relevant to their present or their future, curiosity becomes a powerful ally in the effort to learn. For students to maintain an active interest in learning, they must see the personal value in it. Connecting what they are studying to their world in some tangible way leads them to ask questions and seek answers. If we do not make learning relevant, we are failing our students no matter how many new ideas they are exposed to in a given school year.

In addition to being more likely to enjoy school and participate in their classes, students who believe that their classes are currently relevant are four times more likely to experience support, caring, respect, and enjoyment from their teachers. The effort that teachers put in to making instruction meaningful to the lives of their students creates better connection both to the material being studied, and among the participants themselves.

44% of students agree that "My classes help me understand what is happening in my everyday life." These students are . . .

- 4 times more likely to feel teachers make school an exciting place to learn
- 4 times more likely to say they enjoy participating in their classes
- 4 times more likely to believe teachers care about them as individuals
- 4 times more likely to think teachers respect students
- 3 times more likely to believe teachers enjoy working with students
- 3 times more likely to say they enjoy being at school

. . . than students who do not agree that their classes help them understand what was happening in their everyday lives.

Students who perceive the benefit of what they are learning in school to their future are five times more likely to say they put forth their best effort, push themselves academically, and work hard to reach their goals than students who do not see a connection between school and their future. They are also seven times more likely to believe in the importance of setting high goals. Those that connect school and the future are also 11 times more likely to value good grades than peers who do not see the future benefit of what they are learning. Connecting what is happening in the classroom not only to some general future job or career, but also to each student's particular dream for his or her future, is a far better motivator than external rewards. Recently, a biology teacher bemoaned the fact that she had only learned in April of a student's senior year that the student was planning to go into nursing. "I wish I had known that in September," the teacher said. "I could have provided more individualized reading and homework for her, maybe even created different labs." Students, like all of us, put effort into activities that are or will be personally rewarding. While it is not up to us to dream for our students, we can support their dreams by articulating the links between what we are teaching and how it affects the vision they have for themselves.

79% of students believe "What I learn in school will benefit my future." These students are . . .

- 11 times more likely to believe getting good grades is important
- 7 times more likely to think it is important to set high goals
- 5 times more likely to say they put forth their best effort at school
- 5 times more likely to believe they push themselves to do better academically
- 5 times more likely to say they work hard to reach their goals
- 5 times more likely to say they are excited about their futures

. . . than students who do not agree that they see a future benefit to being in school.

There is perhaps no greater sign of curiosity than asking questions. Indeed, some would argue that the process of becoming educated is not about learning more and more answers, but about developing an ability to ask more and more meaningful questions. Thus, learning becomes life-long. At its most basic, this Condition is about being able to ask "Why?" and "Why not?" Despite the importance of inquiry, one third of students do not agree with the statement "I feel comfortable asking questions in class." This outcome correlates with the school environment's being welcoming and friendly and students feeling accepted for who they are. In the self-consciously charged world of adolescence, students fear looking stupid or smart in front of their peers. Teachers must work diligently to create an atmosphere of trust so that any student at any time feels that he or she can ask any question. In the absence of a question-friendly atmosphere, misunderstandings can accumulate quickly, and as a result some students increasingly fall behind. Perhaps no other factor so clearly demonstrates the connection between the participation and achievement gaps. Students who do not participate by asking questions when they do not understand cannot hope to achieve to the same level as those who ask questions when they do not understand.

64% of students indicate they "feel comfortable asking questions in class." These students are . . .

- 4 times more likely to feel accepted for who they are at school
- 4 times more likely to say they enjoy participating in their classes
- 3 times more likely to think school is a welcoming and friendly place
- 3 times more likely to believe teachers care about them as individuals
- 3 times more likely to think teachers enjoy working with students
- 3 times more likely to believe they push themselves to do better academically

. . . than students who do not agree that they feel comfortable asking questions.

## Deviously Creative

A first-grade student was presented with a question titled "The School Box" on a state assessment. She was asked to draw a crayon box that represented ½ the crayons as blue, ¼ of the crayons yellow, and ¼ of the crayons red. What would you draw? Most students (and adults) would draw two blue crayons, one yellow crayon, and one red crayon. The really ambitious draw four blue, two yellow, two red.

However, the first grader received partial credit with a handwritten comment: "Misunderstood the question." She had drawn five crayons: ½ of each crayon was blue, ¼ of each crayon was red, ¼ of each crayon was yellow.

The challenge in a school or classroom when the focus is narrowly on convergent, pick-the-one-right-answer-out-of-four thinking is that many times creativity and imagination can look like deviance—that is, outside the norm—to a teacher. When standardized testing requires standardized teaching, which requires standardized curriculum, which requires common core standards, it's easy to end up with standardized learning and standardized thinking. Any student not in line with norms seems abnormal.

As you consider the assessment in this story, ask yourself how often you misinterpret originality and creativity as "misunderstood"?

*Source:* Kris Fox.

While the importance of fostering curiosity in students is widely accepted, whether it is the responsibility of our educational system to develop creativity is a subject of debate. While many recognize the importance of creativity, the practicalities of budgets, tight schedules, and high-stakes, standardized testing inevitably squeeze creativity out of schools. Performing and fine art classes are the first cut when money is scarce. Even within traditional academic subject areas, teachers become less creative and less tolerant of creativity, as they work toward covering material in order to prepare students for state tests.

Achievement tests can also affect curiosity in the classroom. In the conclusion of their study of the value of curiosity, Schmitt and Lahroodi wrote, "Achievement tests must emphasize uncontroversial facts and objective skills if they are to be easily gradable, and thus their use tends to crowd out the teaching of controversial subject matter and creative activities" (2008, p. 147). Some see nurturing Curiosity & Creativity as the main purpose of education in our time, while others see both as undefinable, unteachable, and unmeasurable, and therefore not something schools can be responsible for, apart from so called "specials" such as art and music classes.

Most educators we have talked with fall somewhere in the middle. Without fully entering into that debate here, the research makes it clear that students who are encouraged to be creative are more likely to believe they are respected, to feel recognized, and to say they feel supported by their teachers when they make mistakes than students who do not feel encouraged to be creative. They are also more likely to report being engaged, more likely to put forth effort, and more likely to believe they are better prepared for their futures. Craft, who has studied creativity extensively in schools in the United Kingdom writes, "Every good teacher is a catalyst to creativity, a liberator. Every bad teacher creates cages" (2005, p. xiv).

67% of students agree that "At school I am encouraged to be creative." These students are . . .

- 6 times more likely to say teachers help them learn from their mistakes
- 6 times more likely to feel teachers believe in them and expect them to be successful
- 6 times more likely to agree teachers encourage students to make decisions
- 5 times more likely to believe teachers respect students
- 5 times more likely to think teachers recognize them when they do their best
- 5 times more likely to think teachers enjoy working with students
- 5 times more likely to report that they learn new things that are interesting to them at school
- 5 times more likely to believe school is preparing them well for their futures
- 3 times more likely to say they put forth their best effort at school

. . . than students who do not agree that they are encouraged to be creative in school.

Consider this: More than three decades ago in his groundbreaking book *Frames of Mind*, Howard Gardner defined intelligence as "the ability to solve problems or to create products" (Gardner, 1983). In a sense, Curiosity (the ability to solve problems) and Creativity (the ability to create products) are at the very core of what it means to be intelligent. Gardner posited at the time that there were seven distinct kinds of intelligence: Linguistic, Logical-Mathematical, Spatial, Bodily-Kinesthetic, Musical, Interpersonal, and Intrapersonal. He has since added Naturalistic to the list. Yet despite this widely accepted theory of intelligence and its appearance in graduate-level education courses, schools continue to focus narrowly on just two intelligences—Linguistic and Logical-Mathematical. We are led to ask: When will linguistically intelligent students be assessed using music ("Write a jingle . . .") in the same way that musically intelligent students are currently assessed using words ("Write an essay . . .")? When will mathematically intelligent students be asked to dance their knowledge of the Pythagorean theorem in the same way that those students who are bodily-kinesthetically intelligent are currently expected to prove it in numbers?

The moment students enter a classroom their Curiosity & Creativity should be thought of as an intelligence that needs to be cultivated, challenged, and nurtured. To exercise students' curiosity, pedagogy must include questions, conceptual conflicts, debates, and open-ended prompts. Curiosity can be exercised by having students predict story lines, follow news stories, or simply learn about something totally new. To challenge students' curiosity, educators need to guide students beyond their current levels of knowledge. If a student is interested in oceans, then teachers need to provide that student with new and exciting avenues to learn about the ocean. Perhaps that means challenging the student to find a Twitter hashtag related to saving the oceans or to watch controversial documentaries on the environment. Finally, our classrooms can nurture curiosity by teachers and students learning together. Students must see adults continually curious about the world around them and their subject matter. Curiosity may have killed the cat, but it's boredom that is killing our students.

To exercise students' creativity, we simply need to provide students with opportunities to use their whole brain—left as well as right side. Design activities and lessons that use music, art, and different cultures to spark creativity. Challenge students to there-is-no-box solutions to old problems, whether school, community, or world. To challenge and support creativity, develop activities that involve divergent thinking. This involves challenging students to see many possible answers and not just one correct answer. "How many uses can you find for a paper clip" is a classic example, but the Internet is filled with strategies for improving divergent thinking. In addition, allow students to make mistakes. Creativity is nurtured through trial and *error.* Entertain wrong answers. Have students propose "bad ideas" as a solution to some puzzle or problem.

Nurturing creativity also means nurturing the imagination. For example, an elementary school practice around Curiosity & Creativity could involve Show and Tell. Students of all ages love Show and Tell. However, this activity can be structured and connected to whatever lesson the students are learning. It does not have to happen the first five minutes of school merely as a way to allow students to share something about themselves. Ask students to bring something in a brown bag that relates to what you are studying. When it is time for a student to show and tell, begin the activity by letting the class ask 20 questions and try to guess what is in the bag.

Many students are aware of some not-so-pleasant world realities related to poverty and to environmental concerns. As soon as developmentally appropriate, provide students an opportunity to address a community or world problem by building a new invention. Up the creativity ante by requiring the invention to be three dimensional so it cannot simply be written or drawn on paper.

In the high school, ask guest speakers to present ideas, concepts, or even their professions generally. Invite people who have something unique to share about their professions. For example, maybe one guest volunteered in Africa or another might have started a small nonprofit. Break open stereotypes by inviting in a male nurse, secretary, or homemaker and a female truck driver, construction worker, or firefighter. Curiosity & Creativity for all students means constantly challenging not only what they know but also their worldviews.

Beyond the current call from the advocates of 21st century skills that schools teach critical thinking and problem solving, Curiosity & Creativity insists that at the heart of education in every century has been the ability of intelligent people to question, to imagine, to wonder, to explore, to speculate, to hypothesize, and to invent in ways that are natural to them. As the drumbeat for academic outcomes as measured in grades gets louder, let's at least expand what we measure to include all the ways human beings manifest intelligence.

———————————— ⟨⟩ ————————————

## CONDITION 6: SPIRIT OF ADVENTURE

*I love challenging things.*

—second-grade female student

*Last year my teacher asked me to help teach a class. It was so cool, and I think everyone learned a lot.*

—tenth-grade female student

At a recent educational conference, we noticed a prominent theme among presenters: People who are successful develop an ability to "fail fast." Yes, that's correct—if you are going to mess up, better make it quick. All people experience failure along their journeys, but successful people are those who learn from mistakes promptly. They regroup, reflect, and reengage better informed, and better prepared, to achieve their goals. Failing fast is a relatively simple concept if you consider how often we have all called upon it. At its earliest stages, the ability to move on from failure quickly is innate. It would be rather unlikely to witness an able-bodied baby giving up on the idea of walking after one or two tumbles. Consider a 5-year-old learning to tie a shoe or a 9-year-old learning to hit a pitch. Certainly the child's parents and coaches (teachers) would encourage repeated attempts despite the number of miscues. Yet employing this concept seems to become a bit more complicated when engaging in the challenges of school.

The ability—and willingness—to fail is a critical component of having a strong Spirit of Adventure. Students demonstrate a Spirit of Adventure, and behavioral engagement in their learning, when they tackle something new without fear of the outcome—be it failure or success. The student who raises her hand to answer a question even when she is not certain her answer is correct, the middle schooler who approaches a teacher with a concern about an assignment he believes no one in the class understands, and the hockey team captain who auditions for the school musical all exhibit a Spirit of Adventure in their learning.

Whereas Fun & Excitement characterizes emotional Engagement, and Curiosity & Creativity cognitive Engagement, the Condition called Spirit of Adventure describes behavioral Engagement. Though several studies have measured engaged behavior in school as a function of how engrossed students are in a particular task (Yonezawa & Jones, 2009), we define Spirit of Adventure as students' ability to take on positive, healthy challenges, including trying new and unfamiliar things. When schools promote healthy risk taking, students become more confident and resilient. Students with a Spirit of Adventure see life as full of opportunities worth exploring for their own sake.

When talking with students, we have noticed that many of the activities associated with schooling—raising your hand, reading aloud, taking pop quizzes, studying for exams, joining a new club or sport—fall into one of three categories or zones. Students have:

- **A Comfort Zone** where the task is easy, and the student believes she has all the resources needed to complete the task. In the Comfort Zone, breathing is easy.
- **A Challenge Zone** where the task is just outside the student's perceived abilities. The student believes she has *some* of the resources needed to complete the task and believes she can marshal the others. In the Challenge Zone, breathing becomes deeper.

- **A Panic Zone** where the task produces fear and a fight or flight response, and the student does not believe she has the resources needed to complete the task successfully. In the Panic Zone, breathing becomes rapid and shallow.

Engaged learning takes place in the Challenge Zone. Csikszentmihalyi has referred to this state as "flow." When considering the relationship between the level of challenge posed by a task and the level of skill or ability a person has to successfully complete a task, he describes the "flow channel" as running midway between states of anxiety (high challenge and low ability), and boredom (low challenge and high ability) (Csikszentmihalyi, 1990). When a student is in flow, she is actively engaged in the activity, experiencing both enjoyment *and learning* as she engages in it.

Much of effective classroom teaching involves helping students move from the panic/anxiety or comfort/boredom zone into the challenge/flow zone. This pedagogical task is complicated by the fact that the same classroom activity may fall into different zones for different students. Reading aloud may be comfortable for some students, challenging for others, and send still others into a panic that has them asking to use the bathroom just before their turn to read. A further complication is that a student who is normally challenged by math and does well on worksheets may panic on a speed test once the pressure of time is introduced. While we do not want to be overly protective of students, we must recognize that a student who is panicking is too "shut down" to learn. Spirit of Adventure is about creating experiences that are challenging in a way that results in the motivation to learn coming from inside the student. Just as enjoyment is intrinsically motivating in Fun & Excitement, and wonder is intrinsically motivating in Curiosity & Creativity, being challenged beyond one's abilities is intrinsically motivating when it comes to Spirit of Adventure. We see this all the time in young people when they are motivated by inner passions that vary from skateboarding (Sagor, 2002) to gaming (Malone, 1981) to creative writing (Amabile, 1985).

Here is what students report about this Condition in schools.

| SPIRIT OF ADVENTURE STATEMENTS | % IN AGREEMENT |
| --- | --- |
| I like challenging assignments. | 41% |
| I push myself to do better academically. | 84% |
| Students are supportive of each other. | 41% |
| I am afraid to try something if I think I may fail. | 32% |
| Teachers help me learn from my mistakes. | 65% |
| I want to do my best at school. | 88% |
| I am excited to tell my friends when I get good grades. | 60% |

Consider this last result closely for a moment: Students spend at least one third of their waking time either in school or in school-related activities. The measure of success in schools is good grades. Yet, 4 in 10 students do not agree that they are excited to tell their friends they have been successful. Can you imagine similar results if the activities were sports or co-curricular related? Can you imagine 4 out of any 10 high school baseball players who hit game-winning home runs *not* telling their friends if their friends had missed the game? Can you imagine five students getting lead roles in a school musical and two of them *not* being excited to tell their friends?

Having friends to celebrate success with is as important as having peers who are supportive when you are struggling or even failing. A key aspect of Spirit of Adventure is whether students feel support from other students and teachers when they want to try new things. Other people provide a safety net, emotionally and intellectually. If students know where to go for consolation or answers when things don't work out, they are much more likely to take the chances necessary to learn.

Whether students have the courage to move beyond their comfort zone into their challenge zone depends on overcoming fear and anxiety. If students are not willing to challenge themselves and take healthy risks—academically, socially, personally—they do not learn and grow. We have done well in the last few decades as an educational community with making failure a learning experience rather than a cause for shame, however, the data suggest there are more students to reach.

## It Doesn't Matter

A calculus teacher taking one of our Aspirations graduate courses in New Hampshire came into class one day excited to share a story from the trenches. "I think I finally get Spirit of Adventure," he said. "I mean I understand the concept of healthy risk taking and its importance to learning, learning from mistakes and all that. But I was having the hardest time figuring out how to put it into practice day in and day out.

Yesterday we were doing some particularly challenging work in an AP class. As we were going through the worksheet, students were raising their hands giving the answers to problems they had just spent half the class working on. Typical in that class, each student I called on had the right answer.

We came to a very difficult problem and no one raised a hand. I called on one of the better students and she said, "Mr. Douglas, I don't think I have the right answer."

Because I have been thinking a lot about Spirit of Adventure I said, "It doesn't matter." She said, "I don't understand." I said, "Whatever you say, right or wrong, we are going to learn from and that's why we're here—to learn—that's the only thing that matters. If it's wrong, we'll all try to figure out why."

He continued to his colleagues in the graduate class, "That's it, isn't it? It's making it safe for someone to be wrong in the nitty-gritty of something we do all the time, like a classroom check-in on a worksheet."

## IMPROVING THE ODDS

Consider the differences in the odds analysis for students who admit that they are afraid to try something if they may fail. Students who say they are afraid to fail are four times more likely to give up when schoolwork is difficult than students who were unafraid to fail. Students who say they are afraid to fail are twice as likely to be uncomfortable asking questions in class and to believe they are poor decision makers. This strongly suggests that a willingness to risk failure is critical to student success. We must continue to send the message to our students that failure is a learning opportunity and that schools are safe places to learn.

Less obvious, though no less worrisome, are students who are afraid to challenge themselves because they might *succeed*. For these students, having a Spirit of Adventure means a potential threat to their social network—their sense of Belonging—and is therefore a powerful deterrent to success. We see that students who agree that they are excited to tell their friends when they get good grades are twice as likely to say school is a welcoming and friendly place and to feel accepted for who they are than students who are unwilling to share their good grades with their friends. Perhaps these students feel that an already shaky social situation would only be made worse by sharing their academic successes. If all students are to reach their highest potential, schools must find ways to make it safe for students to take on personal challenges and succeed at them.

60% of students agree that "I am excited to tell my friends when I get good grades." These students are...

- 7 times more likely to agree that getting good grades is important
- 4 times more likely to believe school is preparing them well for their futures
- 3 times more likely to believe teachers recognize them when they try their best
- 3 times more likely to say they put forth their best effort at school

- 3 times more likely to believe they push themselves to do better academically
- 2 times more likely to feel school is a welcoming and friendly place
- 2 times more likely to feel accepted for who they are at school

**…than students who do not agree that telling their friends about their good grades is exciting.**

Another explanation for a lack of excitement about sharing good grades could be that some students are disaffected by the entire grading system. There are discrepancies in the survey results between those who are excited to tell their friends and those who are not regarding the stated importance of tests, grades, teacher recognition, academic effort, and the sense that school is preparing them well for their future. Students who are not interested in telling their friends about their good grades may define success differently. Such students may be more excited to tell their friends about a recent athletic, gaming, or artistic achievement or the news about a positive outcome concerning a relationship, even if they get good grades. This brings us back to the need for teachers and schools to recognize all forms of student success.

# Pied Piper

As any middle school educator knows, early adolescence is a dynamic and confusing few years. There is the pressure to fit in, be accepted, and just feel normal. Accordingly, encouraging middle school students to take healthy risks that might result in failure or cause them to "stand out" is not usually an easy task. One middle school band teacher faced this challenge when he tried to get his students to simply try out a new instrument. While the students felt comfortable and confident with their own instruments, they were not keen to try learning new ones.

After exhausting many different coaxing strategies, the band teacher realized that he, and most of his colleagues, spent all day being comfortable and confident with what they taught. At least at school, the students had few, if any, risk-taking role models. So he invited fellow teachers to challenge themselves and step out of their comfort zones for one period over the course of one week.

During this time teachers spent an hour teaching a course totally out of their area of expertise. The PE teaching volunteered to teach chorus. Rumor had it that he was tone deaf. The math teacher, who didn't speak a word of Spanish, taught Spanish. Even the principal taught math, although she was a self-diagnosed "arithmophobe." The students experienced adults pushing themselves, making mistakes, laughing at themselves, and, yes, learning in the process. The following Monday, the band teacher had students willing to try—and perhaps even fail—at playing a different instrument.

The finding that 65% of all students believe teachers help them learn from their mistakes suggests students who fail need more sustained support so they do not give up. We see that when a student feels encouraged in this way, the odds improve that the student believes teachers respect students, care about students as individuals, recognize students when they try their best, and believe in their success. In a comprehensive study of what teachers do to develop intrinsic motivation in students, Reeve concludes, "When teachers use classroom structure to control students' behavior, then students' motivation and learning suffer, but when teachers use the same aspect of classroom structure to support students' autonomy, then students' motivation and learning thrive" (2006, p. 232). Among the positive behaviors he lists as a sign of intrinsic motivation is "a preference for optimal challenge over easy success" (*ibid*, p. 228). In other words, by encouraging students to take on challenges, teachers can improve both learning and classroom management.

While those correlations between teachers helping students learn from mistakes and other perceptions of teacher respect and care are obvious, students who say that teachers help them learn from their mistakes are also four times more likely to say they put forth their best effort and six times more likely to feel encouraged to be creative. Students who feel they have such support in a teacher are also seven times more likely to believe they are being well prepared for their future. This is critical to effective education as even one's best effort can fall short and creativity can end up down a blind alley, so preparation for the future must include lessons in how to pick oneself up when things do not go as well as hoped. Without a trusted guide to help a student overcome errors, the alternative is being stuck in misunderstanding until it is uncovered by another teacher or by life itself.

65% of students agree that "Teachers help me learn from my mistakes." These students are...

- 7 times more likely to think teachers respect students
- 7 times more likely to feel teachers recognize them when they do their best
- 7 times more likely to believe school is preparing them well for their futures
- 6 times more likely to feel they are encouraged to be creative at school
- 6 times more likely to believe teachers care about them as individuals
- 4 times more likely to say they put forth their best effort at school

...than students who do not agree that teachers help them learn from mistakes.

# When Learning Crystallizes

During a recent visit to Wales, I saw amazing sites and learned countless educational lessons, but by far the most treasured lesson was one I relearned firsthand: Teachers have an incredible opportunity and ability to impact the lives of others by getting them out of their comfort zones (observing the work of a teacher), away from their panic zone ("I can't do that!"), and into their challenge zone.

I had the honor of meeting the most talented glasscutter in the world at Welsh Royal Crystal. I was graciously welcomed by the director, David Thomas, and master glasscutter Alan O'Neill. I stood in awe watching Alan work his magic on stunning crystal glasses he was cutting for my dad's birthday gift. I could have comfortably watched him for hours. (Did I mention he personally crafted the Ryder Cup trophy? The crystal trophies at major music awards? Commissioned pieces for the Royal Wedding? Crystal for the Queen?) He is beyond talented, and as I quickly learned, extremely gracious.

Alan noticed the engaged look in my eyes and readily asked if I wanted to give it a try. The look of panic on my face must have said it all: "WHAT? You're trusting me on your treasured wheel? That seat where you have created some of the most memorable pieces of our time? I don't think so." "It's ok," he said, "You can sit here and I'll stand right here." He smiled and pointed to a spot right beside the seat. I had tears in my eyes knowing that the Master of Masters was offering his seat to an absolute novice. I sat down before he could change his mind or I mine!

To say the experience was magical is an understatement—it was life changing. I was enthusiastically invited to work alongside an expert, invited to take a risk and give something new a try. I cut the most amazing crystal glass I have ever seen. In my eyes, it was a masterpiece! Sure, it gave Alan a bit of a laugh, and yes, it was flawed, but the glass Alan and I crafted together sits proudly on my mantel next to various awards I have received. It is a treasure that represents much more than beauty—it reflects the influence a single teacher can have on another individual, at any age. We all have the power to impact the lives of others. All we need to do is extend an invitation—offer a seat, if you will, and stand beside.

*—RJQ*

Schools must also explore how students can be encouraged to champion each other's healthy risk taking. The finding that only 4 in 10 (41%) students affirm that their peers are supportive of one another does not suggest the most favorable environment for learning. Once again there are obvious correlations with perceptions of school as welcoming, friendly, accepting, and respectful, but note also the correlation with school pride. Additionally, those who report peer support are more likely to indicate greater effort and to report greater enjoyment in school than students who do not feel they are in a supportive peer environment. We must remember how important social issues and concerns are for school-age children. Students tell us all the time that the best thing about going to school is that they can be with their friends. They also report that the worst thing about school is not this or that academic struggle, but struggles with relationships (bullying, lack of respect, teasing, a "mean" teacher, etc.). Schools and teachers have a responsibility to create a supportive, safe, and encouraging peer environment not only to socialize students into the niceties of living in a civilized world, but also because there are educational benefits to working in such an environment. Taking the risks necessary to learn is difficult enough without the added obstacle of overcoming fears that one's efforts will result in ridicule.

**41% of students believe "Students are supportive of each other." These students are…**

- 8 times more likely to believe students respect each other
- 5 times more likely to feel accepted for who they are at school
- 4 times more likely to feel school is a welcoming and friendly place
- 4 times more likely to say they are proud of their school
- 3 times more likely to agree they enjoy being at school
- 2 times more likely to say they put forth their best effort at school

**…than students who do not agree that students are supportive of each other.**

Although most educators we speak with are supportive of students as healthy risk takers, they struggle with helping students to actually push themselves. On the one hand, they discuss the straight A students who don't want to risk anything below an A. These students are afraid to take unfamiliar or overly challenging course for fear of their impact on their grade point average. On the other hand, educators tell us about students who are so accustomed to failure that success is a risk. These students are afraid to risk academic achievement for fear of its impact on their sense of Belonging. To support risk taking for both groups, we need to introduce students early in their education to assignments that are not graded. Assignments that simply are about learning and growing should be part of every school

year. Students need the opportunity to learn and push their limits without the often-artificial measure of grades.

Three classroom strategies that support Spirit of Adventure are:

1. Allow students the opportunity to try something new and different and not have it affect their grade. If a student wants to present in front of the class for the first time, then encourage this opportunity with no negative consequences.

2. Introduce students either in person or virtually to those with a Spirit of Adventure. Encourage students to understand the many failures and perseverance that come before success.

3. Model new behavior. For example, if you are not comfortable with technology, try using it your classroom. Share your fear and excitement over this personal challenge.

When it comes right down to it, Helen Keller was right: "Life is either a daring adventure or nothing at all." And to the extent that learning is a fundamental part of life, learning, too, must be seen as a daring adventure. How can schools, which are supposed to be places of learning and places that teach students how to learn, become less uptight and more audacious? How can schools rewrite the script so that they open at the box office not as black-and-white documentaries, but as 3-D

IMAX adventure movies? How do we move away from systems that seem riddled with the fear of failure at all levels toward systems that embrace failure as a necessary part of the process of learning?

## UNINTENDED MISSTEPS AND INTENTIONAL NEXT STEPS

Looking back over the three Conditions that promote Engagement—Fun & Excitement, Curiosity & Creativity, and Spirit of Adventure—we are again reminded that students fail to experience these conditions regularly in school because aspects of the inherited model of school unintentionally block these conditions. Overly strict adherence to pacing guides and curriculum materials leave little room for either Fun & Excitement or Curiosity & Creativity. A fifth-grade student found a snakeskin on his way into school. Thinking this was incredibly cool, he carefully brought the fragile discovery into his first period science class. Excitedly, he said to his teacher, "Look what I found! What kind of snake do you think this was?" To which the teacher replied, "Please put that away. We are not studying snakes this year." We are certain this teacher did not intend to diminish either this student's enthusiasm or curiosity, and yet her need to adhere strictly to what was in the book had exactly that effect.

Teachers may indeed need to follow pacing and curriculum guidelines during class, but nothing we have seen prevents them, when planning lessons, from finding ways to connect what is being learned to their students' interests, passions, hopes, and dreams. Finding the way a math lesson connects to a student's interest in motocross or letting a student do a writing assignment on a fashion designer he admires can go a long way to keeping on track with the needs of both the curriculum for coverage and students for engagement.

Another common practice that diminishes student enjoyment during the school day is the loss of recess or physical education time as schools seek more and more time for instruction in so-called core subjects. Yet we know young bodies need to move, that movement is engaging, and that people learn best by doing. While we cannot comment on the budgetary or scheduling reasons for such changes, it seems reasonable when such decisions have been made to ask teachers to incorporate movement during their classes. Moving periodically during any class improves blood flow, lessens fatigue and boredom, and keeps students literally on their toes. The challenge here is for teachers, who generally *do* move throughout a class period, to become more conscious of students' need to move as well.

The same is true when art and music classes are reduced or cut entirely. Schools and teachers can find ways to integrate art or music across the curriculum. Both stimulate Fun & Excitement, Curiosity & Creativity, and Spirit of Adventure. For some students having to share music that they enjoy or produce a work of art as part of an assessment also involves the risk taking that encourages Spirit of Adventure.

Traditional grading is another challenge for schools and educators who want to promote engaged learning for learning's sake. For a long time we have known about the harm done to intrinsic motivation by external, and seemingly arbitrary, rewards (Deci, Koestner, & Ryan, 2001). Students who become grade conscious tell us in the confidentiality of focus groups that they use a variety of methods to get good grades, from cramming to cheating. Whether it's the second grader who wants the gold star on the top of the spelling quiz more than she wants to learn how to spell or the high school senior who must have an A in history more than he believes he needs to know history, students are not engaged in school in a way that leads to learning. To balance grades, teachers can add narratives and self-reflection to their assessment efforts. Portfolios and journals help reinforce the notion that learning results in products, improved performance, and personal growth, not just in letter grades. Additionally, efforts to assess students based on skills and proficiency and allow them to keep at it until they have mastered material are a step in the right direction.

Finally, the disciplined silos within which students and teachers spend most of the learning day are yet another impediment to engagement. Having students go into a room so that an expert in math can install the widget Algebra II, and then putting them on a conveyer belt (we call it a hallway in schools) so that they can go into a room where an expert in English language arts can install the widget Mark Twain, after which they go back on the conveyer belt so that an expert in social studies can install the widget the Bill of Rights...you get the idea. This is part of the industrial model of school and was an efficient way of educating the large populations of students who began going to school when education became compulsory. Whatever its strengths in terms of efficiency, it has enormous drawbacks in terms of engaged learning.

Students find interdisciplinary and multidisciplinary learning—much of it project or theme based—more interesting. This is the true nature of knowledge and the real world. While there is a time and place for specialization and though many benefits have accrued from it (consider the medical field), as a structure for general education, this segmented model has seen its day. The trend toward real-world and project-based, blended learning is a welcome one and is sure to improve students' experiences of Fun & Excitement, Curiosity & Creativity, and Spirit of Adventure. In the meantime, teachers should find ways to collaborate across disciplines, to team-teach with teachers who have different expertise, and to be deliberate in articulating how the learning in one class relates to learning in other classes and in the real world.

— CRßO —

## CHAPTER 6

# Students Speak About Purpose

*There is kind of an attitude that they are the adults. This is their school. So they don't take you seriously.*

—seventh-grade male student

*Sometimes teachers do something and it has nothing to do with my life, but others make it relevant to your life or what you want to do; you can relate to it.*

—twelfth-grade female student

Far too many students see no connection between their schooling and who they are or who they want to become. Research has shown that this disconnection is a major contributor to the dropout rate. In one study in the *Journal of Personality and Social Psychology,* the authors concluded: "Thus, especially because school tends not to be interesting, students need to find purpose and choice in attending school. Most students generally manage to achieve this end and become motivated out of identified regulation. Students who do not, however, are at risk of dropping out" (Vallerand, Fortier, & Guay, 1997, p. 1172). Earlier in their paper the authors identify "amotivation" in individuals who engage in an activity without any sense of purpose and do not see any relationship between their actions and the consequences of such aimless behavior (Vallerand et al.).

In an effort to counter this trend, many schools and districts attempt to draw links between today's learning and tomorrow's careers, encouraging students to think about their education as tied to the type of work they want to do in the future. There is a significant movement toward Career Technical Education (CTE) and Science, Technology, Engineering, and Math (STEM) schools. While the graduation rate in such schools is up to 15% higher than in traditional schools (see U.S. Department of

Education, 2009a, 2009b), for the most part, these remain niche experiences. Students may be able to attend a separate school or a program within a school, but this approach that connects students' hopes and dreams with their present efforts in school is not a part of the mainstream education being offered by most districts.

Many schools emphasize preparing for college as a purpose of their high school education. This sounds strangely like touting the purpose of school as more school. Seemingly many students see the road to a successful life running through a four-year liberal arts campus. However, Harvard's Graduate School of Education has called into question whether the effort to have every student attend college is serving either our students or our society well. In the report on their *Pathways to Prosperity Project,* they write, "Our national failure to better prepare our young people cannot be explained by poor communications or low aspirations. Rather, the paradox is that even though young people understand they need post-secondary education to make it in 21st century America, huge percentages continue to drop out of high school and college" (Harvard, 2011, p. 9). They advocate a much broader skills-based, real-world approach that leads students to some form of postsecondary credential, but one much more in line with students' own interests and goals.

Throughout a student's "compulsory" K–12 education, schools have a responsibility to challenge students to think about the requirements that accompany successful, rewarding careers or work and the benefits of some form of postsecondary education, *and* they must also encourage students to think about *who* they want to become as well as what they want to do. Reflecting on who they are becoming invites learners to consider their aspirations not just in terms of career, but also in terms of broader, more deeply personal goals. Recall that aspiration is the ability to dream and set goals for the future while being inspired in the present to reach those dreams. Future dreams and the effort to reach them include non-work-related goals for happiness, family, integrity, and making a difference in the world. Reducing school's contribution to the future to merely scholastic (college) and economic (career) consequences would be limiting. Who any person is or is becoming is more than his or her capacity to earn a living. *Who you are* is an expression of your Purpose.

## ■ ■ ■  ASSESS YOUR STARTING POINT

Use the best practices for fostering a sense of Purpose in students below to rate yourself on a scale of 0-10, where 0 is never and 10 is always.

- I teach leadership skills to all my students.

- I involve students in classroom and/or building-wide decisions.

- I discuss school goals and initiatives with my students.

- I use input from my students to improve my teaching practice.

- I have high expectations for all of my students and they know it.

- I talk with my students about their aspirations.

- I teach my students to be reflective.

- My students feel successful when they leave my classes. ∎

In his book, *The Path to Purpose: How Young People Find Their Calling in Life,* Stanford University psychologist and researcher William Damon defines purpose as "a stable generalized intention to accomplish something that is at the same time meaningful to the self and consequential for the world beyond the self" (2008, p. 33). The definition comes out of numerous in-depth interviews with young people who have found, are trying to find, or seem to have no interest in finding a purpose in life. Among the discoveries of his research is that not many young people have a sense of purpose today. Damon writes: "The root of the problem is that, while thinking about their future work, they consider only the surface features of the vocation: what's in it for them, whether or not the work seems like it will capture their interest, the possibilities of fame and fortune, without considering what they are trying to accomplish and how their own aptitudes could be of use to the world beyond the self" (Damon, p. 47). He further states that our educational system needs to do a better job of raising and discussing the issue of finding a purpose for one's life. Thus, Purpose, along with Self-Worth and Engagement, is a Guiding Principle of the Aspirations Framework.

## REFLECT ON YOUR SURROUNDINGS

- What difference do your students believe they can make in their school or community?

- What does it mean for your teaching if you show high expectations for all students?

- How can you use the 8 Conditions to enhance your teaching and learning environment?

- What opportunities do students feel they have to make decisions in your class?

- What authentic decision-making opportunities could students have on a building/district level?

- How could students participate in department or grade-level meetings?

- How do you draw a distinction between *what* your students want to be and *who* they want to become?

- Articulate any differences between student's sense of purpose, your sense of purpose, and the purpose of school.

- How do you ensure that your students are thinking beyond themselves? ∎

Following Damon, Purpose, as we understand it, is composed of intention, commitment, and an ability to think beyond the self. First, students with a sense of Purpose act with *intention;* they are not drifters or idle dreamers. They consciously set and pursue goals that are important to them. They make mindful choices and, for the most part, consider consequences. For students with an academic sense of Purpose, this means being intentional about study habits, note taking, completing assignments, and so on. Students who find Purpose in sports or other athletic pursuits are intentional about exercise, nutrition, and preparing mentally for competition. They consciously push themselves to achieve a personal best in each workout or event. A student whose Purpose is to get a role in the school play is deliberate in her preparation for the audition. Students with Purpose recognize that they will not improve or achieve their goals by accident or coincidence or good fortune.

## COMMIT TO A DIRECTION

- Teach leadership skills to students.
- Involve students in classroom and building-level decisions.
- Discuss local and national politics with students when appropriate.
- Make sure students know you have high expectations for them.

- Seek student feedback regarding their learning and your teaching on a regular basis.
- Co-teach lessons with students.
- Advocate and insist that students have a decision-making role in school that is meaningful. ∎

Second, students with a sense of Purpose make *commitments.* Having intended a particular course of action or outcome, purposeful students stick with initiatives, projects, and efforts related to their Purpose. The greater their sense of Purpose, the greater their level of commitment. Students who see a purpose in going to college commit themselves to doing the necessary academic work, application materials, and financial responsibilities. Students who see a purpose in having meaningful relationships commit themselves to being good friends, to going above and beyond for those they care about. As students mature, these commitments can become lifelong. Furthermore, Purpose drives students to commit to developing the skills and capacities necessary to persist and excel on the course they have chosen. They attend extra clinics, workshops, or classes that help them toward their Purpose.

Third, students with a genuine sense of purpose *think beyond themselves.* They consider others when they act. Purpose draws out the realization that one's actions affect others and that one can choose to be a force for positive change in a community and the world. From the student whose Purpose is to be an outstanding offensive guard and thinks beyond himself to his teammates to the student trying to get into an Ivy League school to become a doctor to help other people, a sense of Purpose leads students to consider how they can impact the people and the world around them. A young person may also have a goal to achieve financial success, but the person with real Purpose considers the altruism financial success makes possible.

## ∞ OVERCOME OBSTACLES

**How am I supposed to instill a sense of Purpose in my students if I don't have it?** You can't! Purpose is as much about modeling intention, commitment, and thinking beyond the self as it is teaching those concepts. Students look to us for not only support and guidance, but as role models. Students need to see teachers who are committed to others and who understand that "who" they are as educators is far more important than what they teach. This in turn translates into a greater sense of "who" I am as a student, not just a person with a grade or class rank.

**Students don't take responsibility for their actions.** They do if we let them and hold them accountable. One mistake is to let students make decisions, and then for the adult to assume responsibility when the consequences are negative. Many school codes of conduct result in adults suffering the consequences of student misbehavior. When we "clean up after"

students, they never learn that their actions have consequences. This encourages irresponsibility. This is more about us as teachers than it is about students. We need to hold students accountable for their actions and, in turn, they will learn to become more responsible. Eventually students become accountable to themselves.

**My students are not lacking in confidence; they are lacking action.** The old adage "actions speak louder than words" could not be more appropriate than in today's society and for our students. So many students believe they are going to be successful but fail to make the connection to the work ethic they need to be successful. Clearly we need to teach students how to establish realistic goals and develop action plans to achieve those goals. Having students with confidence is important, but having them develop a plan to be successful is even more important. ■

Fostering Purpose involves developing students' ability to make positive choices, be accountable, and have confidence. As a guiding principle of Aspirations work, Purpose highlights the importance of intention, commitment, and thinking beyond the self by encouraging student decision making and holding students responsible for the decisions they make. Decisions almost always affect other people in some way and so considering that impact on others should be part of what a school teaches about responsible leadership. In school, students must have leadership roles that carry genuine responsibility for themselves and others. By giving students meaningful leadership opportunities and then holding them accountable to those decisions, schools teach students to choose goals that are meaningful to them and consequential for the world beyond themselves.

## ARRIVE

In schools that develop Purpose in students:

- Students know not only what they are interested in, but also know the kind of person they want to become.

- Students are giving back to the educational community and thinking beyond themselves.

- Students know their opinions are valued and listened to at school.

- Teachers seek student opinions as a regular part of their practice.

- Teachers provide students opportunities to make decisions.

- Administrators offer students diverse leadership opportunities in and outside of school.

- Administrators meet with students on a regular basis to understand their perspective and acts accordingly.

- The community seeks student input into educational policy. ▪

Additionally, schools can and must instill in students the confidence to act in support of their dreams. As educators, we have a profound duty to expect our students to be successful and to support them in the self-assurance necessary to achieve the goals they set for themselves. Talking with a young person who is not excited about his or her future or who has no expectations of his or her future success is deeply disturbing. When students find Purpose in their lives, they have the confidence to take action in order to secure a meaningful, productive, and rewarding future. Schools have a responsibility to prepare students, as Emerson said, "to go confidently in the direction of [their] dreams."

# Discovering *Líderes*

At a school in Mexico, the staff wanted to provide all students with leadership training and skills. The teachers felt their students, who faced personal challenges including poverty, hunger, and transience, lacked these skills due to their home environments. The teachers worked diligently on developing a student conference where students would learn and practice leadership skills, including communication, team-building, and prioritization. Teachers also invited neighboring schools to participate in the leadership conference.

As the conference progressed, the teachers observed something that surprised them—their students were leading students from the neighboring schools. During activities, the students were supporting, guiding, and coaching students who didn't understand an activity or were just too shy to participate. At the end of the two-day event, teachers talked with their students about the experience. While the teachers expected students to talk about the skills they learned from the conference leaders, the students shared that what they liked best was the opportunity to help, to guide, and to support others—in other words, to *be* leaders.

The students also conveyed that they thought no one believed in their ability to be leaders, and that within their communities there were too few opportunities to be positive leaders. This conference gave students a chance to demonstrate—and teachers an opportunity to learn—that students did indeed have the skills but were lacking the confidence and support to be *líderes*.

## CONDITION 7: LEADERSHIP & RESPONSIBILITY

*It's hard to be a leader when you are not liked by other people or you don't have a reputation among the other students. If you're not looked at as somebody who is cool or popular, then you are like cast out and overlooked as a leader.*

—ninth-grade female student

*The principal, she gives us chances to stop making the bad choices we sometimes make.*

—third-grade male student

The work we do in schools frequently puts us in front of school boards to share data and report on the progress of our work, and nearly every school board has a high school student or two on it. The student is usually responsible for communicating the efforts of the sports teams and to announce upcoming student events. At one recent meeting, we noticed that members of the board had name placards in front of them. The student, however, simply had a placard that read "Student." This is typical and a fairly reliable indication that such student "leaders" are tokens and not considered full partners on the board. Could you imagine if the placards belonging to adults had been constructed with descriptors in the same manner—"Middle-aged Father of Two" or "Newest Member" or "Former Classroom Teacher"?

As a Condition that supports a sense of Purpose and makes a contribution to students' aspirations, Leadership & Responsibility is not just about students who become captains of sports teams or end up on student councils. While fostering a true sense of Leadership & Responsibility among students can include such leadership roles, the condition of Leadership & Responsibility invites *all* students to express their ideas, make decisions, and be willing to accept consequences for their actions. It cultivates student accountability for the classroom environment, school community, and the wider community. Schools that promote this Condition teach and expect all their students to be good decision makers. Students are trusted to make the right decisions and are recognized for doing so. Consequences outlined in the code of conduct are not arbitrary or an attempt to deter future infractions, but rather are educational and restorative. While leadership opportunities such as our student board member are indeed valuable, we wish to place more emphasis on the notion that *each and every* student must learn to lead his or her life responsibly.

Leadership & Responsibility in that sense is twofold: First, students must develop strong decision-making skills (visioning, listening, team building, etc.) and second, students must have real decision-making opportunities. Only then can they be truly responsible persons who make a difference in their own lives and in the lives of their community. We look for indicators of these two components of this Condition in the following statements:

| LEADERSHIP & RESPONSIBILITY STATEMENTS | % IN AGREEMENT |
|---|---|
| Students have a voice in decision making at school. | 46% |
| I see myself as a leader. | 67% |
| Other students see me as a leader. | 37% |
| Teachers encourage students to make decisions. | 72% |
| Teachers are willing to learn from students. | 52% |
| I am a good decision maker. | 68% |
| I know the goals my school is working on this year. | 49% |

## IMPROVING THE ODDS

Students who view themselves as leaders and also believe other students see them as leaders enjoy many positive school outcomes. They are more likely to say they put forth their best effort, push themselves to do better academically, set high goals, and work hard to reach those goals than students who do not have an experience of feeling like leaders. They are also more likely to feel comfortable asking questions in class, enjoy learning new things, and believe they are good decision makers. Student leaders are also more likely to feel excited about their futures and believe they can make a difference in the world.

**Students who say both "I see myself as a leader" AND "Other students see me as a leader" are . . .**

- 5 times more likely to believe they can make a difference in this world
- 4 times more likely to say they push themselves to do better academically
- 4 times more likely to think it is important to set high goals
- 4 times more likely to say they work hard to reach their goals
- 4 times more likely to believe they are good decision makers
- 4 times more likely to say they are excited about their futures
- 3 times more likely to say they put forth their best effort at school
- 3 times more likely to feel comfortable asking questions in class
- 3 times more likely to say they enjoy learning new things

**. . . than students who do not see themselves as leaders AND do not believe other students see them as leaders.**

Leadership in the way we are discussing it here is simply about having a voice and a choice in what happens to you. When we talk with students who are struggling and disengaged in school, a significant reason for their negative experience is the belief, real or imagined, that they have little control or influence over what happens to them. From their perspective, they have no input on what they can wear (there is a dress code), where they can go (certain areas of the school are off limits), what they can eat (vending machines have been removed), when they can move (bells ring), or who they can talk to ("Shhhh!"). Students commonly use the word "prison" to describe the institution they believe makes all their decisions for them, including when they can and cannot use the restroom. As educators, we recognize that adults make decisions that get codified in rules and regulations in order to create a school environment that is safe, orderly, and conducive to education. Students tell us that they do not object to rules so much as they object to students not having a say in what rules the school creates or what happens to students who violate the rules. Many students say the rules seem arbitrary and are inconsistently applied.

Student Voice occurs when students are meaningfully engaged in decision making and change-related processes in their school. The effort to give students a voice begins with teachers encouraging students to make decisions in the classroom. These decisions can be about classroom regulations, choice of assignment, options for assessment, homework alternatives, and so on. Just about anything a teacher must decide, she can consider whether the decision can be made by or with students. Recently we saw a very orderly change of class process in a middle school. When the bell rang, students filed out of the class into the hallway and headed for their next class. An arriving group of students lined up in the hallway waiting until the classroom was completely empty before entering. The teacher stood in the doorway and gave the signal when the new class could enter. Our position is that this is something a student could easily be responsible for.

In one England school, we were pleased to observe students providing feedback to both teachers and fellow classmates. Teachers asked students to observe very specific areas of pedagogy over the course of a week in classes the students themselves were not taking. Students willing to do this during a study period or other free time were trained in observations skills and worked with a teacher team and other students to develop rubrics and guidelines. This was not at all evaluative; it was simply feedback to teachers from a student's point of view. For example, in one class, two students were keeping track of student engagement. In creating the rubric, the students determined that high engagement meant that any time a student was called on or asked to participate, he or she was "tuned in." Tuned in also meant that the students appeared interested and were asking meaningful questions. A student who was totally disengaged might be sleeping, acting up, or working on something unrelated to the lesson. At the end of the week, based on their rubric, the students provided feedback to the teacher. Surprisingly, there were lessons that the teacher was sure had engaged most of the class when, in fact, the student observers said many students were working on other assignments. The final step in the feedback process involved working with the students to improve lessons and address instructional elements that appeared to disengage students. Truly this school is a place where everyone, not just students, is seen as a learner.

Student involvement in decision making can occur at three levels: Students can have input and the teacher makes the decision, the teacher and students can decide together, or the students can decide on their own with or without guidance from the teacher. Each level involves some risk taking at first. Both teacher and students must get used to the transfer of responsibilities. There will be a learning curve for both. Not every decision that involves or is turned over to students works out. But that is precisely the point: There will be learning. Students who agree that teachers encourage them to make decisions are seven times more likely to also agree that their teachers help them learn from their mistakes than students who do not agree that teachers encourage them to make decisions.

Some studies show dramatically improved performance in students who have behavioral difficulties when choice is introduced, though little correlation between student choices in the classroom and academic performance in the general education population (von Mizener & Williams, 2009). However, the My Voice results indicate that student decision making is accompanied by a much more positive experience of school. Students who feel encouraged to make decisions have dramatically improved odds for believing their teachers care, respect them, and recognize them. Additionally, the odds increase that such students enjoy classes and learning and feel encouraged to be creative. Decision making often involves imagination and creativity. Finally, and not surprisingly, these students are also more likely to believe that their teachers have an expectation of their success and that school is preparing them well for a future that will inevitably involve many decisions.

# Stepping Up

A student Aspirations Team at one urban high school decided that the traditional step-up day for eighth graders was not comprehensive enough. The Aspirations Team decided that the step-up day needed an activity fair to introduce future high school students to all the clubs, organizations, and sports at the high school.

After much organizational effort, on step-up day the high school students arranged for the eighth graders to visit tables sponsored by various school organizations. Team captains, club officers, coaches, and moderators all staffed the tables. There were trifold displays and photographs and uniforms and sign-up sheets. The golf coach tripled his golf team for the following year, noting, "I am not sure where I am going to get all the clubs . . . but this is a good problem to have." Although pulling off this event was a true display of student leadership, the events that followed the activity fair were what the administration remembered.

An assistant principal shared that as the eighth-grade students were leaving the gym, he saw high school students congregating in the hallways. Panic overcame him as he assumed there was only one explanation for a group of juniors and seniors forming a gauntlet for the eighth graders who were emerging from the activity fair. He encouraged a teacher he was walking with to hasten her steps and they quickly hurried down the hall. However, they were stopped just as quickly as they saw high school students in the corridor high fiving the eighth graders as they left the gym. Hollers of "Get ready for a great year!" and "Welcome to our school!" were heard throughout the hallway. High school students were cheering and clapping as the eighth graders walked through the human arch made by student hands across the corridor. The sending middle school principal reported that his students came back to school on an emotional high and exuberantly shared what had happened.

On step-up day, the Aspirations Team was a catalyst for widespread student leadership at their school.

72% of students believe "Teachers encourage students to make decisions." These students are . . .

- 8 times more likely to say teachers help them learn from their mistakes
- 6 times more likely to feel teachers care about them as individuals
- 6 times more likely to believe teachers respect students
- 6 times more likely to agree that teachers recognize them when they try their best
- 6 times more likely to believe they are encouraged to be creative at school
- 5 times more likely to say they learn new things that are interesting to them at school
- 5 times more likely to believe school is preparing them well for their futures
- 4 times more likely to say they enjoy participating in their classes
- 4 times more likely to think learning can be fun

. . . than students who do not believe their teachers encourage students to make decisions.

That students learn to see themselves as leaders and decision makers, however, is not enough. They must put those beliefs into practice through real leadership opportunities in their school or community. Note that roughly 3 out of 4 students believe teachers encourage students to be decision makers, suggesting the leadership opportunities available in classrooms are a good starting point for greater schoolwide involvement and initiatives. The low percentages of students who say they know the goals their schools are working on this year (49%) or believe that students have a voice in school (46%) are an indication that there is much room for growth here.

Students who are aware of their school's goals are four times more likely to experience greater pride in their school than students who report being in the dark about their school's goals. They are three times more likely to put forth their best effort in school, to see the everyday relevance of their classes, and to feel that creativity is encouraged, and four times more likely to enjoy their classes. Interestingly those students who feel as if they are in-the-know regarding their school's goals also are three times more likely to feel enjoyment and experience encouragement from their teachers. Students who have this fairly simple experience of leadership—knowing the goals of the institution that is such an important part of their lives—feel a greater sense of collaboration with the adults in their school.

49% of students agree that they "know the goals my school is working on this year." These students are . . .

- 7 times more likely to believe school is preparing them well for their futures
- 4 times more likely to agree that teachers help them learn from their mistakes
- 4 times more likely to say teachers encourage students to make decisions
- 4 times more likely to say they enjoy participating in their classes
- 4 times more likely to say they are proud of their school
- 3 times more likely to believe they put forth their best effort at school
- 3 times more likely to believe they are encouraged to be creative at school
- 3 times more likely to feel their classes help them understand what is happening in their everyday lives
- 3 times more likely to believe teachers enjoy working with students

**. . . than students who say they do not know their school's goals.**

That less than half of students believe students have a voice in decision making at school is intensified by the finding that a majority of students see themselves as good decision makers (68%). One traditional avenue of student voice in schools is student council. Yet many students councils we have observed or worked with have become popularity contests in the way they are formed and party-planning committees in the way they work. Nearly all members of the school community recognize this, yet few seem willing to move beyond the status quo. In part, this is because involving students in a school's decision-making process threatens the prevailing power structures. "We have never done it that way before."

Studying student participation in school decision making in a variety of contexts, Frost writes: "There are many opportunities for teachers, senior leaders and those who work with them to support children and young people in participating more fully in the life of their schools and

classrooms. This frequently involves challenges to established practice; however, this need not necessarily lead to increased anxiety and can lead to significant improvements" (2008, p. 365). We have actually heard administrators and teachers say, "We cannot give students that much power." Such a threat to power is one of the greatest limits to change.

An idea we saw for having adults and students share leadership was based on the U.S. Constitution in order to create a "balance of power" in school leadership. The administration was appropriately considered the "Executive Branch" of the school and was responsible for enforcing all school rules, among other things. The "Legislative Branch," responsible for overseeing and creating policies and procedures, was made up of a Faculty Senate and a Student House of Representatives. Faculty elected senators to a two-year term from among a list of student-nominated teachers and students elected representatives to a one-year term from a list of faculty-nominated students. The "Judicial Branch" was a group of five staff members and four students selected by the administration and approved by the legislative branch. Note that this gave the staff a majority bloc for handling discipline disputes, if it came to that, but students seemed to understand and accept this fact. All students learned about this system of government in their social studies classes. Students at this school believed that students had a genuine voice in decision making.

As with the Condition of Leadership & Responsibility in general, student voice is not just about those select few students who are elected to student government having a say, to some degree or another, in the way their school functions. Rather, it is about all students believing that they and other students have a seat at the table where meaningful decisions are made as in the above example. Students who believe they have a voice in decision making at school are more likely to have positive relationships with their teachers—relationships characterized by mutual respect, enjoyment, and encouragement.

## When Students Drop the Ball

In one of the schools where we work, a "type A" teacher (aren't they all?) was struggling with a recent decision to turn over homecoming planning (Spirit Week, a Pep Rally, a dance, etc.) to students. For many years past, teachers, with some student support, had been pulling off a very successful series of events.

The Student Aspirations Team was going to be newly responsible for most of what had been previously done by adults. We had worked with these students and trained them in leadership skills. The school was committed to increasingly moving in the direction of student Leadership & Resonsibility. The teacher and I had the following conversation:

Teacher: I'm a little nervous about this. Homecoming is a big deal. What do we do if the students drop the ball?

Me: *If* the students drop the ball?

Teacher: Yes. If the students drop the ball, what do we do?

Me (feigning): You said, "*If* the students drop the ball?"

Teacher: I don't get what you are asking.

Me: That's because I don't get what you are are asking. You are saying, "If the students drop the ball, what do we do?"

Teacher: Yes.

Me: If? *If* they drop the ball? Can we say "*when?*" *When* they drop the ball?

Teacher: Um . . . sure. When.

Me: Because they are going to drop the ball, right? They are going to make a poor decision. They are going to forget to do something. They will drop the ball; kids almost always do.

Teacher: Right. Okay. When they drop the ball . . .

Me: So, *when* they drop the ball, what will you do?

[Pause.]

Teacher: Teach.

Me: Of course! Never stop teaching, coaching, guiding.

Can you imagine a student tripping over the pronunciation of a word and a teacher saying, "You will never amount to a reader. Stop reading!" Can you imagine a student making a division error and a teacher saying, "Better let me do all the division from here on out." It's unimaginable. When students make mistakes, teachers do what they were born to do: They teach. This is no less true of student leadership than it is of learning Italian or algebra or interpretation of poetry.

—*MJC*

46% of students believe "Students have a voice in decision making at school." These students are . . .

- 4 times more likely to believe teachers respect students
- 4 times more likely to think teachers enjoy working with students
- 4 times more likely to agree that teachers help them learn from their mistakes
- 4 times more likely to feel teachers encourage students to make decisions

. . . than students who do not believe students have a voice in decision making at school.

These data support the notion that the greater the level of student leadership and responsibility and the more students are involved in decision making, the more they feel a partnership with their teachers in the educational environment. The upshot of that partnership is the Self-Worth, Engagement, and sense of Purpose that lead to both high aspirations and high academic achievement.

A school that nurtures student aspirations is one in which adults and students genuinely collaborate. This means all are active participants involved in forming and working toward the school's vision, mission, and goals. It can be interesting to read a school's mission statement and ask whether it is indeed the mission statement of the entire school community—administrators, teachers, support staff, students, and parents—or only the mission statement of the educational professionals in that building. Many we have seen are the latter. This belies a certain assumption about who and what make up a school and an implication, no doubt unintentional, about who is actively involved in living out the school's mission and who is a spectator or passive recipient of those efforts.

--- ⚭ ---

## CONDITION 8: CONFIDENCE TO TAKE ACTION

*People can come out of their shells. I had really low self-esteem, but coming here is helping me change into the person I am now. I don't want to be shy anymore. I want to be a better, stronger person.*

—eleventh-grade male student

*I need to keep my grades up if I want to go to college.*

—fifth-grade female student

The culminating Condition for developing aspirations is Confidence to Take Action. Along with Leadership & Responsibility, it creates the sense of Purpose—intention, commitment, and ability to think beyond oneself—that is critical to student success. Confidence to Take Action is the extent to which students believe in themselves. This Condition is what all effective educators strive for; all other Conditions nurture students to attain this level of aspiration. Confidence to Take Action is characterized by a positive and healthy outlook on life and by looking inward rather than outward for motivation and approval. Schools build their students' Confidence to Take Action by providing support, believing in student success, and encouraging independent thinking and acting.

The condition of Confidence to Take Action is the pinnacle of the Aspirations Framework and the intent of all aspirations-related ventures. We must provide students with enough belief in themselves to set goals for the future and take steps in the present to reach those goals. Practically speaking, this is accomplished when teachers provide the right level of expectations and support in relationship to a student's ability and skill. Among the many applications of game theory to motivation in the classroom (see Przybylski, Rigby, & Ryan, 2010) is the recognition that video-game designers are able to write algorithms that create a perfect and subtle imbalance between a player's skill and ability on the one hand and the level of expectation and support from the game on the other.

What drives the compulsion to play for hours on end (Candy Crush, anyone?) is not so much a craving for pleasure or enjoyment as it is an addiction to the learning necessary to keep advancing and a growing sense of accomplishment and confidence. When the game expects just a little more from the player than his skills are capable of and provides just under the support needed to advance to the next level, the player keeps at it. There is a fairly narrow bandwidth of expectation, skill, and support within which this drive to keep learning occurs.

- Too high expectations (I am at skill level 5 and the game expects a skill level of 8 to advance), and I stop playing.

- Too little support (I have been looking for the key to open the door for hours and it is nowhere to be found), and I stop playing.

- Too low expectations (my skills exceed the game's ability to challenge me) and the game becomes boring, and I stop playing.

- Too much support (the key to open the door is lying right in front of the door) and the game becomes lame, and I stop playing.

While in the classroom it is more art than engineering, the same formula drives student confidence to take action. All educators know that students live up or down to our expectations of them, but expectations must not be so high as to seem unreachable to the student. And having found the right level of expectation, teacher support cannot be so pronounced as to seem like a crutch or so absent that students flounder. We hear from students all the time that the best teachers are the ones who expect more of them than they feel capable of themselves and provide enough support to help them meet their expectations.

| CONFIDENCE TO TAKE ACTION STATEMENTS | % IN AGREEMENT |
|---|---|
| I believe I can be successful. | 91% |
| I believe I can make a difference in this world. | 63% |
| Teachers believe in me and expect me to be successful. | 76% |
| Going to college is important to my future. | 86% |
| I work hard to reach my goals. | 79% |
| I am excited about my future. | 77% |
| I think it is important to set high goals. | 76% |
| I know the kind of person I want to become. | 82% |
| School is preparing me well for my future. | 65% |

The results for Confidence to Take Action are among the highest on the survey. The majority of students surveyed seem to feel strongly that they are capable of achieving their goals. The data does, however, raise three concerns.

## IMPROVING THE ODDS

The first concern is that students' self-confidence is not matched in their eyes by their teachers' confidence in them. This is perhaps one of the most disconcerting findings in the survey. We should note here that there has been a vigorous debate about whether teachers' expectations are correlated with student performance because (a) teachers' perceptions are accurate, (b) teachers' assessment of student work is biased by their expectations, or (c) students live up (or down) to teachers' expectations (Jussim & Eccles, 1992).

**75% of students say "Teachers believe in me and expect me to be successful." These students are . . .**

- 6 times more likely to believe school is preparing them well for their futures
- 6 times more likely to feel they are encouraged to be creative at school
- 5 times more likely to think getting good grades is important
- 5 times more likely to say they enjoy participating in their classes
- 5 times more likely to say they learn new things that are interesting to them at school
- 4 times more likely to say they push themselves to do better academically
- 4 times more likely to feel they work hard to reach their goals

- 4 times more likely to think it is important to set high goals

- 4 times more likely to say they put forth their best effort at school

**. . . than students who do not say their teachers believe in them and expect success.**

Whatever the connection between teacher expectations and student performance, the My Voice survey clearly indicates that when students believe their teachers expect their success, they not only have a more positive experience of their relationship with their teachers, they also work harder academically. Students who trust that their teachers believe in them and expect them to be successful are four times more likely to say they put forth their best effort at school, push themselves academically, set high goals, and work hard to reach their goals than students who do not report that their teachers expect their success. They are also five times more likely to believe in the importance of good grades. "When teachers and school leaders start by conveying to students the expectation that 'they can do it,' what gets interrupted is the familiar cycle of failure and in its place a situation of relational trust is constructed, whereby an ensemble of pedagogical approaches and activities are brought into existence, committed to success" (Smyth, 2006, p. 292).

The second concern raised by the Confidence to Take Action data is that while many students have high hopes for their future success, far fewer believe that school is preparing them well for that future. While the mission statements of many schools speak in noble terms of helping students reach their personal goals, the mission being lived by many schools is that of the school reaching for the goal of ever higher test scores. This is a worthwhile goal so long as the means to achieve it take into account the students' need for Self-Worth, Engagement, and Purpose. We must also squarely face the truth that a student doing well on any kind of test should be a *means* to the end of achieving his or her personal and academic goals, not vice versa.

Though they are the ones taking the tests, very few students share or even know about the goal of making adequate yearly progress (AYP). This disconnect between the current aspiration of many schools and the aspirations of students may be why students do not feel school is preparing them well for their future. When schools focus on preparing for standardized tests, students, who have in mind a standardized test-free future, do not feel they are being adequately prepared for that future. This is also the very reason schools cannot close the academic achievement gap by focusing solely on academics. If we are honest, the very reluctant buy-in of the teachers preparing students for the tests is only slightly higher than the buy-in of the very people who take the tests. This makes it difficult to move the academic-achievement-as-measured-by-standardized-tests needle much further than it has already been moved.

Students' goals in school, which include academic goals, are much broader and more varied than those expressed in AYP. Society itself has a wider set of goals for its young citizens than those measured by high-stakes testing. Unlike the adults working with them, many students do not care at all if their school makes AYP or not. Even the most academic among them are more interested in test scores for personal reasons, like getting into college, than institutional ones. Yet making AYP has become the nearly single-minded focus of all the adults working with students.

## Up a Creek

Students at a continuation high school on the West Coast are doing more than simply recovering the credits they need to graduate; they are stepping up as leaders for positive change. Watching them happily show up for volunteer "creek cleanup" on a Saturday morning or make a confident presentation to city officials to ban plastic bags, you might not guess that these students previously struggled to find purpose in school.

For most, regular attendance and classroom participation were real issues. Now, however, they can cite with poise an impressive and ever-growing list of accomplishments, from building and maintaining an organic garden in what was once a weed-filled lot behind their school to helping provide clean drinking water to communities across the world. What accounts for their transformation?

While students are quick to describe the incredible sense of Belonging they now feel at school ("We are like a family"), they credit their school for providing them with the opportunities to take on real-world issues with local organizations. In doing so, they are able to apply the things they learn in hands-on, relevant, and engaging ways. As a result, they have bloomed into responsible citizens and young, passionate leaders. And as anyone who meets them can attest, their enthusiasm for improving the world around them is absolutely contagious.

*Source:* Halo Smart.

Note that students who report that school is preparing them well for their future are 10 times more likely to agree that getting good grades is important! Clearly students see the importance of positive academic outcomes when they believe that the educational efforts they are engaged in will matter to their future. Believing that school is preparing them for the future, students are much more likely to put forth effort, push themselves academically, and work hard to reach their goals. Educators who wish their students to believe that school is preparing them well for their future must learn their students' goals, inspire their students to work hard to reach those goals, and help students see the connection between school and the fulfillment of their dreams. When this connection is made, as it is for some, effort, engagement, creativity, excitement, and even grades, follow.

**70% of students believe "School is preparing me well for my future." These students are . . .**

- 10 times more likely to think getting good grades is important
- 7 times more likely to agree that they learn new things that are interesting at school
- 7 times more likely to think teachers help them learn from their mistakes
- 5 times more likely to feel they put forth their best effort at school
- 5 times more likely to say they enjoy participating in their classes
- 5 times more likely to believe learning can be fun
- 5 times more likely to feel they are encouraged to be creative at school
- 5 times more likely to say they push themselves to do better academically
- 5 times more likely to agree that teachers encourage students to make decisions
- 5 times more likely to feel they work hard to reach their goals
- 5 times more likely to say they are excited about their futures
- 4 times more likely to say they enjoy being at school

**. . . than students who do not believe school is preparing them well for the future.**

The third concern raised by the Confidence to Take Action data is that despite nearly all students believing they can be successful (94%), far fewer believe they can make a difference in the world (63%). While perhaps indicative of a society that disconnects individual success and making a difference for others, this gap, in such a young population, is troubling. Adolescents tend to be idealistic. Yet here, the disparity between their own anticipated positive prospects, and the world's benefiting from their success, implies a cynicism or self-centeredness that is disconcerting.

With Confidence to Take Action we have come full circle and back to the very definition of Aspirations with which we began. There is a profound difference between dreaming about the future and taking the steps needed to reach those dreams. The condition of Confidence to Take Action is defined by the successful integration of these two processes. The relationship between the previous 7 Conditions and the outcome represented by this eighth Condition cannot be overstated. These connections are worth examining across all three Guiding Principles.

Students who agree with both statements "I think it is important to set high goals" and "I work hard to reach my goals" have a dramatically different experience of school than those who do not agree with either statement.

Students who agree with both "I think it is important to set high goals" AND "I work hard to reach my goals" are . . .

- 15 times more likely to think getting good grades is important
- 10 times more likely to feel they put forth their best effort at school
- 3 times more likely to feel school is a welcoming and friendly place
- 3 times more likely to say they have a teacher who is a positive role model for them
- 3 times more likely to feel teachers care about them as individuals
- One third less likely to say they give up when schoolwork is difficult

. . . than students who do not agree that it is important to set high goals or to work toward their goals.

Clearly there is a correlation between relationships, recognition, and resilience and students having confidence to take action. Our current approach to assessment and accountability has ignored or obscured this connection for far too long. Effective teachers feel this connection every time a student responds with increased attention to the use of her name instead of "dear," every time a student athlete does well on a quiz following that teacher's attendance at a game, and every time a student gives greater effort in a class that began with five minutes of checking in. The bottom line in the results is that students who set goals and work toward them do so because they are grounded in experiences of Self-Worth.

# Getting Bold-er

Student council members at an urban elementary school decided to step up and take action when they learned that almost everyone in their building thought the cafeteria was too noisy and a stressful place to eat lunch. They came up with a creative solution: A Boulder Garden.

They mapped out a plan for a boulder garden that would include four large benches, boulders that could also be used to sit on, and a flower garden in the center. The boulder garden would have seating for 25 students at a time, enough to accommodate an entire classroom. They felt that the boulder garden would provide a peaceful place for teachers to take their classes for lunch (on a rotating basis), and doing so would reduce the number of students in the cafeteria, thus making it a quieter space. They also thought the space could be used for classroom lessons.

By placing the boulder garden at the front of the school, students planned to alleviate a second common concern: crowded hallways during dismissal time. With many parents picking up their children, the students felt that the boulder garden could be designated as a safe waiting place.

Student council members decided to make their plan a reality by applying for a local, youth-led service grant, which awarded them $500 for the project. Student council and local garden club members collaborated to build it. Once the boulder garden was completed and classes had a chance to use it, students resurveyed the school to find out if their effort had a positive impact on cafeteria noise and hallway congestion, as well as to learn from teachers if it was working as an outdoor classroom space. All agreed that the boulder garden had accomplished both.

## CONFIDENCE TO TAKE ACTION AND ENGAGEMENT

Students who set goals and work toward them are more likely to be engaged in their classes than students who do not set goals and work toward them. They are more likely to enjoy school, their classes, and learning. They are more likely to report that their teachers are engaging, help when they make mistakes, and have high expectations of them. Relevance in both the present ("My classes help me understand what is happening in my everyday life") and the future ("What I learn in school will benefit my future") is also more likely in those students with Confidence to Take Action. We also see a high correlation between this confidence and academics: students who integrate goal setting and the effort necessary to reach their goals are 10 times more likely to push themselves to do better academically. This is no doubt because in a school setting, among the goals students set for themselves are academic goals. In an extensive study of goal theory, Covington writes that students' "adopting learning goals was positively associated with deep-level processing, persistence, and high effort, a combination that also led to increases in achievement" (2000, p. 177).

Students who agree with both "I think it is important to set high goals" AND "I work hard to reach my goals" are . . .

- 10 times more likely to feel they push themselves to do better academically
- 6 times more likely to say they enjoy learning new things
- 5 times more likely to believe that what they learn in school will benefit their futures

- 5 times more likely to say they enjoy participating in their classes

- 4 times more likely to believe learning can be fun

- 4 times more likely to say they learn new things that are interesting to them at school

- 4 times more likely to say teachers help them learn from their mistakes

- 3 times more likely to say they enjoy being at school

- 3 times more likely to think teachers enjoy working with students

- 3 times more likely to believe teachers make school an exciting place to learn

- 3 times more likely to feel they are encouraged to be creative at school

- 3 times more likely to agree that their classes help them understand what is happening in their everyday lives

- 3 times more likely to report that they are excited to tell their friends when they get good grades

. . . than students who do not agree that it is important to set high goals or to work toward their goals.

## CONFIDENCE TO TAKE ACTION AND PURPOSE

Finally, students who both set and work toward goals see themselves as leaders, are much more likely to believe their peers see them as leaders, and believe they are good decision makers. Goal-oriented students are more likely to believe school is preparing them well for their futures and more likely to be excited about their futures. They are also more likely to believe they will be successful. If that is not a reason for supporting student aspirations, we don't know what is.

Students who agree with both "I think it is important to set high goals" AND "I work hard to reach my goals" are . . .

- 11 times more likely to believe they can be successful

- 10 times more likely to say they are excited about their futures

- 7 times more likely to think going to college is important for their futures

- 6 times more likely to think school is preparing them well for their futures

- 5 times more likely to feel they are good decision makers

- 4 times more likely to believe they can make a difference in this world

- 4 times more likely to think teachers believe in them and expect them to be successful

- 4 times more likely to say they see themselves as leaders

- 3 times more likely to think other students see them as leaders

**. . . than students who do not agree that it is important to set high goals or to work toward their goals.**

Schools that instill in students the confidence to act in support of their dreams are fulfilling the deepest purpose of schools: to help each and every student become the best possible version of him- or herself. The road map for each person's best possible self is his or her aspiration. From that map, teachers and school leaders must take on their roles as guides. Educators must encourage in students the capacity to imagine a fulfilling tomorrow, inspire them today to take steps toward those dreams, and, motivated by that imagination and inspiration, develop the willingness to achieve in school as an integral part of reaching their goals. We must keep moving toward the day when the success of our schools is measured, not only by their ability to produce proficient test takers, but also by their ability to persuade students of their value and the value of other human beings, to promote in students engagement in the lifelong process of learning, and to produce in students a sense of purpose that makes their lives and our world the better for their efforts.

## UNINTENDED MISSTEPS AND INTENTIONAL NEXT STEPS

Very few people would expect a school or classroom to be co-governed by adults and students as we do. Students' sense of Purpose has the potential to grow when they exercise autonomy and self-regulation. Most Codes of Conduct we have seen have the effect of transferring the consequences of student misbehavior to adults. A student is late and as a result a teacher must interrupt class, deal with the disruption at the door, follow-up with administration, and perhaps even oversee a detention or make up work. It was the student who made the mistake, but an adult that suffered most of the consequences. Somehow adults have become responsible for monitoring student behavior, catching student good deeds and misdeeds, assigning arbitrary

carrots (rewarding good behavior) or sticks (traditional, arbitrary consequences), and managing follow-up. In the real world, when someone bangs his head against the world that person gets a headache. In schools, it's as if a student bangs his head against a wall, an adult gets a headache, and then steps on the student's foot to teach him a lesson about not hitting his head!

A high school in Montana was having problems with students coming late— late to school, late to their next class, late getting back from lunch. They gathered their student leaders and asked them what they thought should be done. "Stop ringing the bells," the students said. This was counterintuitive for the adults. As adults, our solutions would be to ring the bell louder or longer, to put teachers in the hallways to hustle students along, to have some kind of zero-tolerance at the threshold. The students said, "Stop ringing the bells. The school tried it for one month to see what would happen. Not ringing the bells virtually eliminated the lateness problem. Most students at that school now arrive early to class, chat with friends or the teacher, organize their work, or read a book while waiting for class to begin. Everyone arrives where they are going when they need to arrive.

Why did this work? Because it shifted responsibility from an outmoded system largely governed by adults to the students. The students rose to the expectation that they should be on time. Not ringing the bells worked because every student in that school had a cell phone (cell phones synchronize time just as the bell did) or was with someone who did, and was willing to be responsible for being on time.

A similar and common misstep is found in blanket rules that remove responsibility for particular behaviors from individual students and place them on students in general. Because some students cannot self-regulate their use of mobile devices, mobile devices are banned. Because some students cannot behave on field trips, there will be no field trips. Again, these may seem like sensible solutions, but we must point out how such generalized approaches fail to teach students to learn proper behavior in particular and ultimately affect learning.

Rather than ban cell phones, what if schools had an appropriate use policy and students who did not adhere to the policy had phones simply taken away and handed back when the period was over? We heard of one student leadership group that solved and enforced such a policy on their own with Red Zones (completely off limits; e.g., bathrooms), Yellow Zones (classrooms when a teacher allowed students to use devices for class or when the lesson was over but time remained), and Green Zones (the cafeteria, senior lounge, and so on). Not wishing the threatened total ban if the new policy didn't work, the students self-managed the policy. Because this school had a good process for student voice, all students ratified this system and committed to it.

When students are invited to develop classroom rules instead of being told the rules by the teacher, when they are given choices in what to read or how to review instead of being assigned study material, when they are allowed to disagree agreeably with an adult decision and not be outranked by the teacher and made to feel inferior, students learn Leadership & Responsibility and the Confidence to Take Action.

---

CR80

# PART III

## LEADING

## CHAPTER 7

# Students as Co-Leaders

*Every week I would have all of the classes go into one room so we could talk about how you feel about something. Like, why is your behavior like that; why would you do something like that? I think this could help our problem with bullying.*

—third-grade male student

*School is our community, and we're not in charge, but our voices should absolutely be heard.*

—eleventh-grade female student

When some people hear about Aspirations work or student voice, they make the mistake of thinking that this is the "soft" work of school, as distinct from—or for some as opposed to—the "hard" work of teaching the academic disciplines. Some even relegate Aspirations work to guidance or make it the sole province of an advisory or homeroom period. While we believe that every aspect of school life is open to Aspirations work, the best practices we have seen integrate the 8 Conditions into everything from teaching practices to discipline policies.

Schools that recognize the importance of student voice and that adopt Aspirations work implement improved transitional year programs and enhance orientation in order to develop students' Self-Worth. They change school schedules to make room for Engagement so that class does not end just as it gets interesting. They revise tardy and absence policies to put more, not less, responsibility on the students in order to develop a sense of Purpose (rather than the adults-having-more-responsibility approach of trying to punish lateness out of existence). Schools that adopt Aspirations as a framework begin to look at everything they do through the lens of the 8 Conditions. Do our school celebrations improve Sense of Accomplishment? How will this new writing curriculum inspire Curiosity & Creativity? Does our discipline code promote Confidence to Take Action in our students and staff? This is far from "soft"; in fact, it is among the most challenging efforts a school can adopt.

While the ways in which schools implement the Aspirations framework vary, they share one thing in common: effective leadership. Deep, difficult changes to a school's policies and procedures flow from the effective leadership of administrators, staff, *and students*. Meaningful changes occur when adults and students become partners and together lead the school in a direction that benefits all.

We play a game in schools in which two teams try to solve a mazelike puzzle. We map a grid out on the floor with tape and stand the two teams on opposite sides. We make clear that there is only one safe path through the "maze" (i.e., safe squares) and explicitly state that the goal of the game is for both teams to get safely through the maze. And though there is nothing in the rules that implies competition, the two teams nearly always play as if they are opposed to one another. The only real solution is for the teams to cooperate, to work together, and to share what they are discovering from both sides of the maze. What one team is learning can benefit the other team and vice versa. They must solve the puzzle together to uncover the one path that they can both safely use.

Schools are filled with similar mazelike puzzles. Why do students think teachers "yell for no reason" when they are being appropriately corrected in what seems like a calm tone of voice? Why are students disengaged despite hours of preparation by the teacher? Why is the purpose of school unclear even though the school's mission statement hangs in every classroom? Like the game, there is only one safe path: Teachers do not intend to be disrespectful and students do not want to be disrespected. Students do not want to be bored and teachers do not want to be boring. Most schools have clear mission statements, yet most students have no idea if they are its agents or its objective. (Read your school's mission statement and see if it would make sense if a student read it aloud.)

Also like the game, rather than "compete" in opposition—if students win, adults lose; if adults win, students lose (think cell phone or dress code policy)—adults and students must be co-leaders in the effort to improve their school. Only by seeking win-win solutions in partnership can we hope to solve many of the puzzles confounding our schools. As we encourage schools to allow students to meaningfully lead change with adults, some have said, "You want us to turn the asylum over to the inmates." Besides being an interesting metaphor for school, the comment reveals a lack of understanding about partnership.

Use the best practices for being a co-leader with students to rate yourself on a scale of 0-10, where 0 is never and 10 is always.

- I collect, organize, and share student input with my colleagues.
- I invite students to observe decision-making groups of which I am a part.

- I allow students to self-assess their work and progress.
- At least once a week, I eat lunch with students to better understand their perspectives on my class and our school.
- I share and discuss school goals with students.
- My students know I expect them to be leaders. ■

There are different teams in all organizations and institutions: surgeons and nurses, manufacturing teams and sales teams, actors and stagehands. To say they are partners does not mean that stagehands appear in front of the audience. To be effective, teams act in cooperation, not opposition. Nurses exercise leadership *as nurses* and surgeons *as surgeons*. The nurses do not perform the surgery. If manufacturing and sales do not cooperate, businesses lose money. If schools continue to "play" school as if students and staff are in opposition, we will continue to lose students and come no closer to solving our problems.

An elementary school in Appalachian Ohio was struggling with a chaotic start to every lunch period. No manner of adult command or control could get the students to behave as they raced from class and jostled for position in the lunch line every day. Even the normally well-behaved students seemed caught up in the unwelcome crowd mentality. Because they were working on increasing student voice, the administrators decided to sit down with the students to try to find out what was going on together. They learned that the melee was caused by a new lunchroom procedure that required students to file directly from the serving line where they had received their food on trays into bench-style cafeteria seats. This meant that if a student wanted to sit with friends at lunch, he or she had to get in line with them *before* entering the serving area. Coming from different classes, it was a mad dash to find one's friends and get in line with them.

Members of the fourth-grade student voice team, teachers, and lunchroom personnel "came together in the middle of the maze" several times to formulate ways to improve their lunchroom so that students could sit with their friends and which included expectations for proper cafeteria behavior (e.g., busing trays, keeping noise levels down, and so forth). Once expectations and procedures were established, the leadership group shared them with teachers, students, and cafeteria workers. This new plan was so successful, the school expanded it to all grades. Some problems simply can't be solved until we entertain the students' point of view.

Leadership is the key to this approach, but the door must be unlocked from both sides. As never before because the world is as never before, the door needs to open wide to the truth that students must have a voice. In *The New Meaning of Educational Change*, Michael Fullan asks the question: "What would happen if we treated the student as someone whose opinion mattered in the introduction and implementation of reform in schools?" (2007, p. 170). While he wrote that in the first edition, he goes on to add in the fourth edition that "Little progress has been made since the first edition [of his book in 1982] in treating the student as a serious member of the school" (p. 171). We would submit that not only has this question gone unheeded since it was issued, but the situation now is more dire.

## Teaming and the Three Rs

In our work in Canada's schools, we were fortunate to partner with passionate, committed educators. In an effort to improve student engagement, one middle school decided to start team teaching every Friday. The concept of team teaching was not new; however, they took it to a new level by comprising teams of two students and a classroom teacher. On Team Teaching Fridays, they partnered to work on the "3 Rs": Review, Rearticulate, and make it Real.

The teams met for planning on Thursdays during lunch. On Fridays, the teachers began by reviewing the content for the class. After the teacher's review, one student would rearticulate the material in a more student-friendly way. This often included revamping a lesson through the use of videos, guest speakers, and interactive games. The second student, charged with making it real, had to either connect the week's learning to lessons from another class or to real-world experiences, jobs, or news events.

For example, one week a class studied poetry. On Friday, after the teacher's review, the students decided to rearticulate what they learned by sharing songs that were similar to the type of poetry they had learned during the week. Then they made it real by sharing poems written by teenagers around the world in war-ravaged cities. The students led a discussion about how poetry gave these teenagers a forum to express their feelings, despair, and hopes.

In our time, there is a particularly new conflict between students' experiences of being "voiceless" in schools and their experience of their voices outside of school.

We live in a Facebook world, a "Twitterverse," an Instagram, Blogger, YouTube age in which students freely voice their unfiltered thoughts unhindered and uncensored. Those thoughts and podcasts and videos and artwork and multimedia creations may endure in clouds and on servers for decades. Students are more used to having a voice than they ever have been before. For many students, the six to seven hours they spend at school are the only time they are voiceless. The challenge for those of us who are adults and who seek to lead in this partnership with students is not that they are unprepared or unwilling to have a voice. They are quite practiced at putting their thoughts and opinions and feelings out there for the world to see and hear. The challenge may be that we are not prepared or willing to listen. In part that is due to the deafening cacophony of competing voices from academics, from researchers, and from policymakers.

## THE CURRENT CACOPHONY

As attempts to lead school reform have unfolded themselves in various programs and initiatives a curious thing has happened. We hear all the time we are in an amazing place in education. We only wish we knew where it was! As educators we must be careful not to fall victim to a new psychological disorder called *educational schizophrenia*.

Educational policymakers talk about the importance of having an educational system based on *trust and responsibility*. Yet every time we are in schools they seem to be living in a *testing and accountability* environment. You don't need to go very far in the education world to hear proclamations of "we need all time learning, everywhere, in every way" by some of the most influential educators of our times. This is brilliant. Why then are students feeling smothered in schools with new textbooks and more standards, regulations, and guidelines?

Conflicting messages rage on in politics when both sides of the aisles claim schools need to ensure:

- 21st century skills, yet get back to basics;
- social cohesion, as well as cultural diversity;
- academic achievement, as well as vocational relevance;
- freedom from politics, yet responsibility to public clients; and
- sensitivity to national needs, yet responsiveness to local citizens.

Seriously, can someone just take a deep breath and look at the insanity of what we are trying to do?

How will we conduct ourselves as leaders in order to harmonize this cacophony of voices? Without something to help pull it all together, we run the risk of becoming not just a fragmented profession, but dis-integrated professionals. The current effort to create a common focus in academic outcomes is failing. We have reduced assessment to measuring acts of the head and what counts the most to merely academic achievements. One reason for this is that most of those calling for assessment, developing assessments, and analyzing assessments tend to be cerebral sorts. In a sense, consciously or not, they are trying to clone themselves. Another reason is that academic assessment is fairly easy to do. Despite its being nearly 30 years since Howard Gardner proposed that there are "multiple intelligences," despite a growing body of research about the need for educating for "emotional intelligence" and "social skills," despite repeated appeals for a "whole child approach," and despite the call that our world needs an education system for "a whole new mind," as we write this *adequate yearly progress* is still primarily defined by a school's performance on academic metrics alone.

# My Plate Is Not Big Enough

Do you ever feel like you have too much on your plate? We are not referring to mealtime, but to the plate of life. We have been hearing this a lot lately—people bemoaning that their plates are too full—so we considered: How did we get to this place? Whose fault is it that we have so many servings on our plate simultaneously? And the real question: How can we make sure our plates do not overflow?

We think we reached this place because we chose to let the servings pile up and overflow. We know some of you are saying, "We have no choice but to accept the items that are placed on our plates." We say that we do. Our advice is simple: Don't be gluttonous—simply say "NO." Be selective, prioritize, and even be polite, but say "no" to unwanted servings, and soon you will see your portions reduced. If we do not learn to refuse certain servings, then the overflowing plate is our own fault.

If an item happens to appear on your plate when you're not looking, and you find yourself stuck with it, then it is time to reassess and remove something. Is there a secret plate rule that says once something is placed there it must stay forever—even if it goes bad and spoils? That is crazy thinking! Your plate is only so big, and there is only so much that can get piled on before things start falling off and making a mess.

In the buffet of educational reform, we seem to be gorging on everything offered. We beg you to stop, look, and assess the options in front of you before filling up on more. There are countless opportunities to choose from, and even if they are all good for you, you can't appreciate the value of each one when they are mixed into an overflowing mess. Make conscious choices and create room on your plate for the things that matter most. For those of you who do not heed this advice, but rather continue to load up your plates with everything that is on the menu: either get a bigger plate or eat faster, but stop bellyaching.

This path toward having no child left behind as we race to the top (does anyone else see the irony in the United States' two prevailing educational policies?) is having modest success toward the single-minded goal of raising test scores. But there are unintended and unwelcome consequences in the school personnel being asked to implement the effort and in the students meant as the beneficiaries. We have met many teachers and administrators who say they are being sucked into systems that operate at odds with their core beliefs and values as educators. This is dangerous and a recipe for widespread burnout.

# This Ear Bud's for You

It so happened that in the spring of one school year, two separate schools we worked with had a similar problem: too many students in ISS (in-school suspension). Not only were the numbers too high, but they had increased over the school year and now seemed out of control. In both schools, this was frustrating to the adults as more and more students missed class and fell behind. In both schools, adult solutions of lecturing or becoming either stricter, or at times more lenient, only led to greater frustration and even distrust—an inevitable outcome of an inconsistently enforced code of conduct.

Both schools were far enough down the Aspirations road that each had an Aspirations Team of staff and students. This team is meant to model for a few years the kind of partnership we hope to see throughout an entire school system at some point. So the team in each building took on the challenge of ISS.

In both schools, the teams studied discipline records to see why most students were in ISS. In one, they noted that most students were receiving this consequence for being written up three times for minor infractions. They further noted that most of the write-ups were for violations to the school's restriction on the use of earbuds and texting in the hallways (both considered safety issues). So now they knew why students were in ISS, but why had it increased over the year? Why wasn't the punishment a deterrent? One student on the team said, "Duh. You get to listen to your iPod or use your cell phone in ISS."

Sure enough, the moderator of the ISS allowed this as a way of keeping students helpfully under control. So if you were the kind of student who wanted to listen to music so badly or text someone so desperately that you were willing to violate a school rule to do it, all you had to do was get caught three times and then you could do it all day! It was only the students and adults working in partnership that led to a different and more unpalatable form of ISS that was able to solve the problem.

In the other school—a high-pressure academic charter school—the cause of the increasing ISS was entirely different. The records revealed an abundance of fairly major things that resulted in ISS, from mouthing off to a teacher to disruptive behavior in the classroom. Not only that, whereas the demographics ISS at the one school had mostly frequent flyers, the charter school's ISS demographics were diverse and included students from all over the school, including what teachers would call "good" kids.

What the students at this school were able to introduce into the conversation was the fact that when students felt behind academically, they purposely did something to get an ISS. For them it was an entire day you could spend getting caught up. This was a profound eye opener for the staff. Together the students and teachers worked toward solutions that would help students who needed to catch up—without using ISS to do so.

When school board members never interact with students because "they can't vote" (this was actually overheard), when superintendents govern school districts from behind desks because they are buried in an avalanche of paperwork, when principals feel compelled to cheat so that their schools will make adequate yearly progress so as not to lose funding they desperately need to serve their students, when teachers "teach to the test" despite knowing that no real learning is taking place, something is gravely wrong with the system, not with the people in the system. While recent calls to use value-added assessments in order to reward effective teachers and remove ineffective teachers may be research-based and well-meaning, they do nothing to alter the fundamental assumption that academic performance scores as measured on standardized tests a few days a year are the sole valid measure of success.

Let's be perfectly clear: The fault for the current fragmented approach is not with the thousands who have given their lives to the noble endeavor of educating children. No matter what role we play—administrator or classroom teacher, school nurse or parent volunteer—the pressures pushing and pulling us in every direction, the endless parade of programs we are asked to adopt and implement, and the lack of a coherent policy as one administration and then another and then another tinkers with schools "for the sake of our children and their futures" are what have us and our students disconnected from our aspirations to make our communities and the world a better place.

Where does that leave us? How do we, together with our students, lead out from (the meaning of *educate*) this situation and into a more coherent one? We do not enjoy a common understanding of who we are as a society, so the idea that schools should socialize students cannot be a unifying force. A common vision of the future cannot unify education because we do not currently share a common vision of the future in our country. Nor are the academic disciplines a unifying force. They vary in their content and pedagogy. Some would say teaching in discreet academic disciplines is part of what is wrong with the current approach, making it seem as if learning and knowledge itself is fragmented.

Our position, perhaps obvious by now, is that the place it all comes together is in the student. Specifically, each child's ability to aspire—that is to say, each child's innate desire to experience, understand, know, and decide more and more in an ever widening spiral as he or she matures and grows—can and should be the foundation of all our educational efforts. Even as the disciplines expand and society changes, the human capacity to aspire—to set goals and work toward those goals— remains relentlessly constant. Human aspiration is what causes the academic disciplines to expand and the greatest hopes for our society's future to come to fruition. In schools, this means that each student's aspirations and the Guiding Principles and Conditions that support those aspirations must be a driving force in everything a school does. If it is unacceptable that the primary purpose of schooling is merely to produce effective test takers, we can think of no better primary purpose than that schools be places where each student is provided with the conditions necessary to dream about his or her future and the inspiration to work toward that dream in the present.

## REFLECT ON YOUR SURROUNDINGS

- Given the incredible number of initiatives in education, how do you understand what matters most?

- What is your current experience of school like as an administrator, teacher, school staff member, or parent? Does the educational schizophrenia described in this chapter resonate with your experience? How is it similar? How does it differ?

- What do you do to create clarity in what you do on a daily basis in schools?

- How does Aspirations, as you currently understand it, fit in with other theories of education you have read about or studied? How is it similar? On what points does it differ?

- How can you change the way you teach and/or interact with your students to allow you to stay true to who you are and at the same time capitalize on the concept of student aspirations?

- What are some of the concrete implications of attending to the implicit curriculum, the whole child, or students' social and esteem needs? ∎

## CHAPTER 8

# The Context of Leadership

*Community helps you learn. If our community is all focused on the same thing, we're doing it together.*

—eleventh-grade female student

*Being a leader means showing people what happens if you show respect to friends and teachers. So, other students know what could happen if you do something good.*

—second-grade male student

I f we are effectively to lead *with* students and on behalf of students, we would do well to situate our Aspirations efforts in the broader context of four of the more influential ideas shaping education today. While numerous policies and programs have come and gone over the past half century, three seminal ideas have endured, and one current movement is actually grounded in the more traditional wisdom that to be successful one must communicate, collaborate, think critically, and be innovative.

## ASPIRATIONS AND THE WHOLE CHILD

Aspirations is squarely in the camp of educators who seek to make students the center of the educational enterprise. Though children are different and have different needs, that we ought to be educating the whole child—head, heart, and hands—seems to be common ground. Few would argue that what sits on the carpet square or in the desk or at the computer is a whole child, not just that child's head or left frontal lobe. There may be quibbles about priorities (Does hands-on learning lead to better head learning? Can we get cognitive results without affective engagement?), but there is an integrity in the whole child that holds the promise of reversing the dis-integration that has taken hold. This trend in education has its fullest expression in the work of Maria Montessori and the school movement that bears her name.

The Association for Supervision and Curriculum Development (ASCD) lists the Whole Child approach as one of its major programs and initiatives. Articles promoting the Whole Child philosophy appear regularly in the ASCD's widely read journal, *Educational Leadership*. Chief among the tenets of the whole child approach are ensuring and encouraging a healthy lifestyle, creating and maintaining a safe and intellectually challenging learning environment, actively engaging students in their learning through a variety of instructional strategies, providing each student with personalized learning, and preparing students to be college, work, and life ready.

The Aspirations Framework is in harmony with this set of ideas and practices. Like whole child approaches, Aspirations invites schools to attend to the teaching and learning environment as a critical factor in developing positive learning outcomes. Like whole child approaches, it seeks to make the voice of students an important partner in all conversations having to do with classes and the life of the school. Like whole child approaches, Aspirations ultimately seeks to have each student develop the capacity necessary to be the agent of his or her own learning and to lead his or her life with confidence and conviction.

## COMMIT TO A DIRECTION

- Co-teach lessons with students.
- Invite students to actively participate in grade-level and department meetings.
- Make students responsible for organizing and leading parent conferences.
- Seek student input regarding school rules and discipline.
- Provide opportunities for older students to welcome and orient all new students to the school.
- Develop an STPC Association (Student, Teacher, Parent, Community). ■

## ASPIRATIONS AND MASLOW'S HIERARCHY OF NEEDS

Those who would seek to lead Aspirations work must consider the psychological needs of the whole child. Most educators are familiar with Abraham Maslow's Hierarchy of Needs. The initial study of exemplary people published as *A Theory of*

*Human Motivation* in 1943, has had a significant impact in education and schooling. His findings basically help us recognize that human beings have needs that must be met in a certain order if they are to learn or, as Maslow would say, achieve self-actualization.

Maslow's hierarchy is often portrayed as a pyramid with five levels. At the most basic level, people's needs are physiological. They have a need for food, water, shelter, sleep, and so on. Once those needs are met, they have certain safety needs—personal security, order, predictability, and protection from harm either intentional or accidental. Following those, human beings have social needs. These include a need for acceptance, for support, for friends, and for affection. In short, people need other people. The fourth set of needs has to do with esteem.

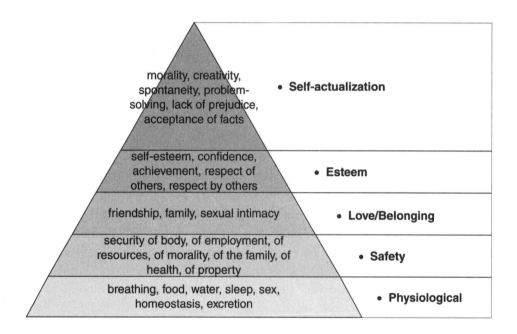

Esteem, according to Maslow, involves being accepted and valued by others. Esteem includes both the respect of others and self-respect. Finally, human beings have a need for self-actualization. People have a desire to be creative, to solve problems, and to be able to deal with spontaneity. Self-actualization also includes moral and ethical needs and the concerns of just and equitable living. Later revisions of his schema have added cognitive and aesthetic needs between esteem and self-actualization, and a need for transcendence beyond the need for self-actualization.

Aspirations themes find an affinity with all of Maslow's needs. Most obvious is the connection between the guiding principle of Self-Worth with its implementation through Belonging, Heroes, and Sense of Accomplishment and young persons' social and esteem needs. One way to help students feel that they Belong and have Heroes is to provide for their physiological and safety needs. Indeed, at the basic level, and among the most obvious and pervasive consequences of Maslow's work and others like him, is the free and reduced-price lunch program and the proliferation of programs that provide breakfast to students before school starts.

Additional connections can be seen between the Engagement Conditions of Fun & Excitement, Curiosity & Creativity, and Spirit of Adventure and the cognitive and aesthetic needs of students. As Aspirations research shows, students have a hunger for relevance in their educations and a thirst for school experiences that are meaningful and applicable to their daily lives. In addition, student creativity (an aesthetic need) seems to be given short shrift in many schools. Finally, developing a sense of Purpose in students by encouraging Leadership & Responsibility and Confidence to Take Action are in accord with Maslow's belief that we all have a need for self-actualization.

While the 8 Conditions cannot be strictly assigned to one level or another of Maslow's hierarchy, both sets of research support the notion that students learning, growth, self-actualization, and aspiring are enhanced when schools work on students' self-worth, engagement, and sense of purpose. The two approaches—one from the field of psychology, the other from educational research—support the idea that academic achievement and the effort to improve the emotional, personal, and social environment go hand in hand.

## Aspirations as Curriculum

In a school, any leadership effort to reach children wholly, address their psychological needs in appropriate order, and work toward each student's aspiration must eventually consider the school's curriculum. Curriculum is where the desires of adults to teach and the desire of students to learn come together. One way of understanding where Aspirations fits into the life of a school is to look at it in terms of Elliot Eisner's (1994) work on curriculum theory. Eisner taught us that there are actually three forms of curriculum:

1. The Explicit Curriculum

2. The Implicit Curriculum

3. The Null Curriculum

The explicit curriculum is what gets taught by *what* we teach. Typically, it is instruction in the academic disciplines: math, English, science, history, social studies, etc., and their accompanying objectives, rubrics, and assessments. When a school holds a curriculum night for parents, the explicit curriculum is typically put on display. Also in this category would be any character education or behavior management programs used to teach and talk with students about "Honesty" or "Respect" or some other agreed upon value or virtue.

The implicit curriculum is what gets taught by *how* we teach and *who* we are when we are teaching. The implicit curriculum cannot be found in books (though there is an implicit curriculum between the lines of any book), but rather in the many thousands of incidents and interactions that take place during a school day. The implicit curriculum is subtle and very powerful. It is also far more pervasive and persuasive in a school than the explicit curriculum. Everything a school does teaches at this level. Students are learning something whenever the public address system clicks on with an "Excuse the interruption. . . ." A school that has done away with recess has taught something implicitly. Being in a block schedule teaches something. The school dress code teaches something. The way a school spends money and allocates resources teaches something. Whether or not a school takes seriously the voice of students sends a message.

The implicit curriculum teaches more effectively than the explicit curriculum. No matter what the student handbook explicitly states as the dress code, if and how it is enforced and by whom will teach something far more profound. We have heard countless stories of inconsistently enforced discipline policies that teach lessons about fairness and favoritism and that undermine teacher morale. If the exciting explicit curriculum of the breakthroughs in genetics is taught with a droning monotone, genetics becomes boring. Even if a school has a student government, the kinds of decisions they are permitted to make teach something different and possibly at odds with the explicit fact that the school has student leaders. Ralph Waldo Emerson captured the power of the implicit curriculum beautifully when he wrote, "Teacher, I cannot hear what you are saying because who you are speaks too loudly."

## X = Y

Mr. John Flaherty must have been about 60 years old. We thought he was 100. He was a wiry, fastidious algebra teacher who had been teaching for nearly 40 years. He was rumored to have been a Golden Glove boxer back in the day. He had wisps of greying hair on the sides of his balding head, wore dark-rimmed reading glasses off the tip of his nose, and donned a white lab coat covered in yellow chalk dust (remember chalk dust?).

He would clutch a clipboard against his chest, rock back and forth heel to toe, and when you made a mistake, say things like, "Mr. Corso, your mother loves you. But it is a moral obligation." We would murmur to one another, unsure if we were being complimented or insulted. He insisted on neatness in presentation, on-time homework, and careful display of all steps in the process of working out an equation.

*(Continued)*

For two years, I sat in his class and earned straight As. He was an outstanding algebra teacher. I was an outstanding algebra student. Today there is one sure fact: I don't know any algebra. I remember almost nothing Mr. Flaherty taught me in the explicit curriculum. But I remember *everything* else Mr. Flaherty taught me that was in the *implicit* curriculum. To meet deadlines. To work diligently until a problem is solved. To be on time. To *always* be prepared. Mr. Flaherty never stopped teaching algebra to teach us how to use a planner, he just expected us to be prepared. It was *who* he was and *how* he taught that taught us the most.

—MJC

Aspirations work lives and has its effect at this powerful level. Some schools adopt Aspirations as an explicit curriculum and this is appropriate, especially in the early days of doing Aspirations work. They teach students *about* Belonging, they discuss who their Heroes are, and they teach Leadership skills and what it means to behave with Responsibility. This approach makes Aspirations work nearly indistinguishable from the many character education programs that seek to improve school climate and student behavior.

But schools that adopt Aspirations as a *framework for action* recognize there is a far deeper place to go. Beyond teaching about Belonging, there are policies, practices, norms, and customs that either accept people for who they are or exclude them. Beyond teaching about Heroes, there is the effort to be a Hero by attending or inquiring about sports and performing arts events or practices. Beyond having a discussion about Accomplishments, there are schools that revise report cards to reflect an accurate assessment of student progress, effort, and accomplishment and not just provide a single-letter, end-product, merely academic grade. Implementing Aspirations does not mean interrupting a math lesson to discuss current events in order to be relevant so students will be engaged, and then going back to teaching math. The idea is to spend five minutes at the start of each math class having students find math in the daily newspaper in order to implicitly convey the relevance of math.

We cannot bully students into not bullying one another and seriously expect that we have taught them not to bully. We cannot disrespectfully correct students who are being disrespectful and think we have taught them a positive lesson about respect. We cannot encourage creativity by pointing out how creative an answer is while at the same time not "counting" the out-of-the-box approach because it didn't follow the rubric. Forty-five years after Marshall McLuhan coined the phrase "the medium is the message," this would seem like common sense, but we have seen a far different set of common practices.

If we are to successfully nurture our students' aspirations, we must not only promote the vocabulary of the 8 Conditions, we must also make it the grammar, the logic, the very framing structure of what we are doing. The underlying pattern of interactions, at times explicitly referred to, is the vehicle (what *curriculum* means in Latin) that needs to carry the Aspirations message. We are talking about a school's infrastructure—the rules, written and unwritten, which govern how people behave and engage with one another. Do students raise their hands in class or are Popsicle sticks with names pulled from a jar at random? Is art a separate class or integrated into the rest of the curriculum or both? Is the discipline code consistently applied or is it applied variously by teachers or (worse?) applied variously to students? Do the students who win top honors at a drama festival receive as much fanfare as the athletes who win their division? These are challenging questions that, if we are serious about wanting to improve school for students, demand solutions even more challenging to implement.

The third and final form of curriculum is "the null curriculum." According to Eisner, this is what gets taught by what we leave out or choose to ignore. An example of this is the fact that most U.S. history books do not mention the fact that Meriwether Lewis, famed explorer, naturalist, and hero of the American frontier, committed suicide. The null curriculum in this case teaches us that our heroes do not commit suicide. In some schools, students' aspirations are part of the null curriculum, never receiving any mention or attention. This contributes to the conclusion of many students that school has no connection to their everyday lives—in which they are starting to work toward their futures—and only a vague connection to their futures.

## ASPIRATIONS IN THE 21ST CENTURY

Leadership that supports Aspirations is about educating the whole child while considering their needs in a way that takes seriously the power of the implicit curriculum to shape what students learn. While the tried-and-true 20th century ideas of Montessori, Maslow, and Eisner continue to withstand the test of time, leaders must also consider our present context. Now that we are well into the new millennium, there is a consensus that the skills required to be successful in the 21st century include: communication, collaboration, critical thinking, creativity, global awareness, and technology (see www.p21.org). We should consider, however, that though what is meant by technology has changed (at one time, the printing press was new technology), those are the same skills that would have made someone successful in any other century!

Of greater interest than *what* skills are most useful in our time (or at any time) and whether and how they are explicitly taught in schools, Aspirations is primarily interested in *how these skills are practiced and lived by schools.* In order to discover whether these skills are being taught, one need only review a school's curriculum. But in the rush to raise proficiency, performance, and implement 21st century goals, all too often educators neglect the perspective of those who belong squarely in this century and no other—their students.

## OVERCOME OBSTACLES

**We have student leaders, but they do not represent all of our students.** When schools begin to partner with students, the obvious and easy route is to work with students who are organized, well-behaved, and get good grades. This is a well-intentioned mistake. All types of students from the introverted, quiet students to the ones who seem to have residency in the principal's office have something to teach us and have the potential to lead. Educators need to be aware of their own biases when choosing student leaders or designing systems to choose student leaders.

**Our students already know how to lead.** It might seem strange to list this as an obstacle, but it is assuming your students know how to lead that can get in the way. Depending on students' experiences and skills, they may need some leadership training. In most cases, we make assumptions that if we put a student (or anyone) in a leadership position, they automatically become one. We have learned that training on problem-solving, creative thinking, communication, and listening skills—not to mention a good dose of confidence—are among the most needed for students.

**Change that involves students as leaders creates too much resistance for staff.** Change is hard for everyone. Educators who have never considered co-leading with students are often resistant to the thought of working with students as partners. There is little doubt that it is actually easier to teach alone. However, easy doesn't mean right. Teaching with a student will not only be an incredible learning experience for the student, but one for the teacher as well. Leading with students will benefit the student and the whole school. Each and every time we develop this partnership, mutual respect grows out of the experience.

Giving students a voice to this extent is "turning the asylum over to the inmates." As a school moves toward a system that partners with students, often teachers start to feel that their voice no longer matters. "What about us?" is a common statement we hear from staff members when we have been working on student voice. School leaders need to be cognizant of this dynamic and take the time to also listen to the concerns and ideas of their staff even as they listen more widely and deeply to students. Increasing student voice without at the same time increasing staff voice is like trying to drive a car with the parking brake on. It can be done, but not for long or without doing damage. ∎

Let's begin with *collaboration*. Here there are two issues. First, the inherited traditional model of school is grounded in a competitive, Lone Ranger approach to education. Individual desks in rows for individual study to take individually administered tests resulting in individual grades on individual report cards was, and in many schools still is, the norm. In this mode, group projects are a sporadic and often inconvenient ("How do I grade this?") concession to the need to teach students to work together. The most common form of student-driven collaboration in this traditional approach is something the grown-ups call "cheating." And if our focus groups are any indication, such "collaboration" is rampant. Interestingly, among the adults, schools have shifted to a more collaborative, teaming approach and professional learning communities are increasingly the standard for professional development, not the exception. But has our approach to student education followed the same collaborative trend?

Second, while in many schools collaboration does take the form of students learning to work together on academic projects, the adults in schools that undertake Aspirations work must meaningfully and effectively collaborate with students. When teachers and the systems of a school make collaboration between adults and young people an implicit part of their everyday lives, then students are learning more than just how to get along with peers. They are learning about collaboration in "the real world" of the school and school decision making, not just in the more or less manufactured environment of a project. In the real world, collaboration is intergenerational, with participants playing various roles, some of them hierarchical.

Employees must learn to work collaboratively with supervisors, not just obey them. Information, insights, and judgments of fact and value must flow in two directions regardless of differences in experience, rank, or age. These lessons cannot be learned if the only collaboration students experience in school is with those who share approximately the same year of birth. Belonging and Heroes are fundamental to collaboration. In addition, students report that collaboration is a significant source of Fun & Excitement.

If collaboration between adults and students in a school is to be genuine, *communication* is necessary. Communication involves the ability to listen to others, be heard by others, and express your ideas both orally and in written form. While one would hope high schools graduate students with this ability, college professors and business leaders alike lament the lack of communication skills in today's graduates. Skilled communication requires opportunity and practice. Together collaboration and communication are about students having a voice. Student voice drives Aspirations work and is a necessary part of Leadership & Responsibility. Many high schools actively seek and utilize student voice in order to help every student reach his or her fullest potential. The positive results connected to student voice include school improvement, civic engagement, and positive peer relationships (Fielding & Rudduck, 2002; Mitra, 2004).

Communication is not just about speaking, but also about listening. We hear all the time that effective leaders listen. And that listening is a form of respect. But listening is a skill that is rarely formally taught in schools. We explicitly teach the other three communication skills—reading, writing, and speaking— but not listening. And having learned a lesson from Eisner, we must ask how well educators teach listening by modeling it? Having spent nearly a quarter century encouraging student voice, we wonder if we should have spent more time developing adult ears.

## Talk Is Cheap and Listening Is Cheaper

During an end-of-year visit to one of our schools in England, we were disappointed and surprised to learn that the Student Aspirations Team had disbanded. At the beginning of the year, the student group was excited and eager to make a difference in the school. In the first few months, seemingly more students signed up to be on the team after each meeting. The students developed insightful ideas based on My Voice survey results, student focus group feedback, and talking with peers. They were ready for action.

However, as they began to present their ideas to the principal, they were met with mistrust and resistance. Ideas were shot down and never given the opportunity or support to grow. Students were not given any space or time to meet other than after school, even though many of them belonged to clubs or played sports that met after school. With every setback, a few more students dropped off the team. In talking with staff members, we learned that school leadership was not ready to learn from and with students. Listening to students is easy; it's *acting* on what they say that is a price not everyone is willing to pay.

*Creativity* is an important topic in education and for our economy. Graduates rarely enter a job market that requires simply rote work. Our successful friends in other fields seldom report being required to choose one right answer from among four. Even in manufacturing more innovation is required than in the past, as line workers are routinely asked how they might improve production. That the jobs of the future require innovative thinkers has been well established. Our world needs students to solve complex problems from different perspectives. Creative thinkers like Steve Jobs and Nobel Laureate Professor Yunus, who developed the successful and impactful

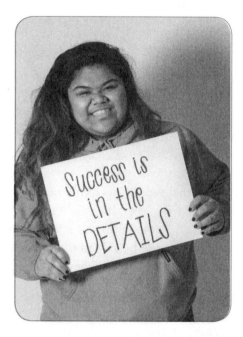

micro-lending business in Bangladesh, change the world. The Condition of Curiosity & Creativity stands at the center of Aspirations work and encourages in students a mindset that is critical to their future success. Moreover, as co-leaders students must bring their innovative solutions to the real problems facing their school. We have seen students propose numerous solutions in schools in which adults felt stuck. Students have effectively designed new schedules, created new discipline consequences, planned new traffic patterns in cafeterias, and even developed new teaching strategies.

The term *global aware*ness includes the notion that students are able to work with people from diverse cultures in a respectful and collaborative manner. In our interconnected and interdependent world, this skill befits a range of concerns from world peace to being able to work effectively with colleagues in a multicultural environment. A prerequisite to the respect necessary in a multicultural world is that students experience respect in school—most students' first exposure to diversity. Fostering the Conditions of Belonging and Heroes in a school elevates the importance of diversity beyond the issue of tolerance to one of respect and

celebration. Being taught about global awareness is one thing, living in the awareness of and reliance on the diversity that makes us stronger as a school community is another. Learning a skill, 21st century or otherwise, is well and good; practicing that skill in the microcosm of the real world that is the school is better still.

As recently as five years ago, you could hear teachers debating the role of *technology* in the classroom. Should students be allowed to use the Internet for homework? Should the school have a Facebook page? Is cyberbullying our concern? Should I let my students follow me on Twitter? What's a Twitter? Given the pace of technological change, these debates seem already quaint. (Although we recently heard a teacher declare: "The reason I don't allow students to use cell phones in my class is because when students get in the real world, they are not going to be able to use technology the way they want." We're not sure to which real world this teacher was referring.)

Although we have seen an amazing growth in the use of technology in schools ranging from Smart Boards, podcasts, and interactive online learning, schools still lag behind the culture of youth when it comes to technology. Many of the reasons schools cannot keep pace have less to do with resource constraints than with discomfort and an unwillingness to let go of traditional methods. We have heard students appreciate the new interactive whiteboard in their classrooms but bemoan the fact that only the teacher gets to use it. Mobile devices have become the new front in the adult rule-making versus student rule-bending that seems a perennial part of the school experience. Most schools have a cell phones out-of-sight policy (is a cell phone being used under a desk to text out of sight?). But one school we know has a cell phones in sight policy. Upon entering a classroom students place their mobile devices (if they have one) on their desk. Teachers may use them during class (e.g., to do a calculation, to look something up, to Tweet something out), and the device being in sight prevents any unsanctioned use. If we can't keep up with the technology, we can allow our students to use technology to learn in a way and at a pace that suits them. Students' proficiency with technology also creates a wonderful opportunity for them to teach us.

We believe students learning 21st century skills is as much about *how* the school functions as it is about what it teaches. When we teach students skills—communication, collaboration, technology—but do not allow them to practice those skills in school—"I didn't ask for your opinion," "You need to stop talking to one another," "Put away that cell phone"—we send a mixed message. What is actually learned is what we *do,* not what we *teach.* We must provide not only classes in creativity, collaboration, communication, global awareness, and technology, but also we must provide the opportunity for students to be creative, work together, make meaningful decisions, respect one another, and use the technology that is such an embedded part of their world. And at the risk of being redundant, all of these skills must be applied not only in ways that are merely academic, but also in a partnership between adults and students in order to lead real school improvement.

## CHAPTER 9

# From Student Voice to Our Choice

*Teachers who are open-minded to your thoughts, opinions, or what you have to say—that shows respect, when they want to hear what you have to say.*

—eighth-grade male student

*If teachers listen to what I have to say, I want to listen to them.*

—ninth-grade female student

When taken together, our own investigations and the work of the influential thinkers point toward a common approach: Putting at the center of what we do in education, the student and the student's need for a learning environment that supports his or her need to develop Self-Worth, be Engaged, and form a sense of Purpose. Montessori and Maslow teach us that the heart of education is the heart of each and every child. Eisner and the effort to promote 21st century skills teach us that our work must include the implicit curriculum—the school's policies, procedures, norms, and customs—if we hope to have a meaningful impact on our students' lives.

In our time, there really is no other philosophy of education that is tenable. The disciplines can no longer provide a manageable governing structure. As high schools, in particular, cling to this traditional way of structuring school, they are showing signs of stress and, in the worst cases, obsolescence. In literature, the list of classics grows every day and an emerging global awareness is expanding the canon far beyond its traditional, Western boundaries. History and social studies, too, are massively impacted by global interconnectedness and political upheaval. The rate of change in science is even more dramatic. High school teachers can barely keep up with the ever-expanding edges of the discipline in quantum mechanics or genetic biology. In many schools students know more about technology and computers than their teachers do. This trickles down into elementary schools in the form of increasing time spent in academic programs at the expense of recess and other free-time opportunities during which students also learn important lessons. Those who look to the disciplines for coherence are being quickly overwhelmed.

Nor is there a single agreed upon view of society that can provide the sought for harmony. The ongoing and irreconcilable debate over values education is enough to show that without a common vision of society, a common vision of how to educate for society is nearly impossible. Beyond a certain small agreed upon set of values, there is no comprehensive social philosophy or ideology available to schools to align the multiplicity of efforts. We live in a time when lawsuits have been brought against saying the Pledge of Allegiance and holiday celebrations and decorations have been banned. Even though much of the control of schools remains in the hands of local communities, those communities themselves are increasingly heterogeneous and sometimes divided.

Schools need a solid foundation on which to build. If that foundation cannot be the academic disciplines or society (either as it has been or as we hope it to be), that foundation must be the student. More concretely, it must be the voices of *your* students. Recall that we define student voice as occurring when students

are meaningfully engaged in decision making and improvement-related processes in their schools. When students participate in this way, schools change and improve. When only adult voices are heard and considered, as they have been, the status quo remains intact. You are now faced with a decision.

We have shared with you the voices of more than one million students from every type of school and walk of life. They do not always speak in a harmony. Their message can at times seem mixed. Some have told us they know teachers care about them as individuals and others have said that teachers do not even care if they are absent or not. We have heard from students who believe they are encouraged to be curious and creative and those who claim they are bored beyond belief. Together we have listened as many students reported confidence in their own abilities, even as some report their teachers do not share that same confidence in them. Despite the disparities, these have been the voices of your children—whether an A student or Alt Ed., whether jock or goth, whether fully parented or unparented or a teenage parent themselves. If you are an educator, all students are entitled to the full measure of your efforts to develop their Self-Worth, Engagement, and Sense of Purpose.

We are convinced that one of the many things that keeps the status quo in place is "analysis paralysis." Schools are inundated with data. Administrators and teachers are asked to process and act on test scores and international trends, demographic data and dropout rates, state averages and Department of Education statistics. The numbers can become numbing. We are inviting you to place one set of numbers above the rest: The numbers that most directly represent your students' experience of school. Not what they can achieve or how they compare with students abroad or whether they have reached some standard. Those numbers are important, but not primary. They are *outcomes* of how our students experience school on a daily basis. In particular, they are the outcomes of students who believe in themselves or don't, students who are meaningfully engaged or passively spectating, and students who have a sense of purpose or drift.

When we can clearly distinguish the effect (academic achievement) from the cause (students having aspirations), we can no longer ignore the magnitude and significance of what has been reported here. The odds analyses clearly show the impact of students' perceptions about their learning environment on their motivation and academic efforts. Students across the country have spoken and we need to listen—and, having listened, we need to act. The preceding chapters not only shared data with you but hopefully have challenged you to reflect on your role in education and to be honest with what your own experience is witness to.

As we reflect on what we have found and reported in this book, we find ourselves tossed about in the turbulence, not only of numbers, but also of political rhetoric about our schools. With a combined half-century working in education, we are frustrated by the fact that current educational reform agendas must be translated by someone with a law degree and that the educational research on which they are based can only be understood by a sophisticated postdoctoral student fresh from course work on chi squares and kurtoses. In our bureaucratic rush to test anything with a pulse, we have lost sight of the face at the other end of the stethoscope—our students. Not seeing them, we run the risk of missing the real mark, which is drawing out each and every student's fullest potential.

## ARRIVE

In schools in which students and adults co-lead:

- Staff meetings are designated as "school meetings" where students present and participate in decision making with staff on a regular basis.

- Students open the school year with the administrators. Student leaders review student management policies with students, explain changes to the curriculum or rules, and introduce new staff. In such schools the message is clear that school belongs as much to students as it does to adults.

- Students have several official seats on the school board. These should be elected positions just as they are for the adults on the board. Once elected, there is a training module for students (as there should be for the adults!). Students have a vote. They serve two-year terms beginning in their junior year. Students should only not be allowed to participate in situations where there is an absolute need for confidentiality.

- Students and adults attend state-level meetings and conferences as participants—not just to play in a band or be part of some other Let's-Show-Off-the-Students event.

- Students are part of the interview process for all staff, including administrators.

- Students plan college and job fairs.

- Students plan step-up days, open houses, art fairs, etc.

- Students (of all ages) meet regularly with the superintendent to discuss district/school goals. ◾

We—and in this "we" we trust we can include you—did not embark on careers as educators to improve standardized test scores, to follow endless regulations and directives in lock-step, or to meet the constantly moving target of adequate yearly progress. All of us want each of our students to reach his or her fullest potential, to do well academically, and to be contributing citizens in today's society. But the challenge to ensure a quality education for every student has left teachers and administrators across the country inundated with guidelines that are stifling even to the most talented. In the government's quest to ensure that there be "No Child

Left Behind" and to encourage a "Race to the Top," they have left all of us trailing in a wake of numerical abstraction and regulatory obstruction. The particular and real students that walk into your school every day, *they* are the reasons we became educators. We are confident that their voices can help us sort out a way to reach each and every child.

If you are like us, you became an educator to make the world a better place. We believed that we could actually influence the future by teaching students some content, while at the same time showing them we cared about them as people. As we see it, we have three options:

1. We can leave the teaching profession. Many have done this. According to *No Dream Denied: A Pledge to America's Children,* written by the National Commission on Teaching and America's Future, one third of new teachers leave after three years and nearly half (46%) leave after five. Teacher retention is a growing problem, especially in high-poverty areas.

2. We can remain a puppet in the system. This is another option chosen by many. Most quietly go about their work, grateful that most of their day is spent with the students they entered the profession to serve; content to gripe behind closed doors about this new program meant to raise reading levels or that new initiative started to improve math scores; adopting what they think will work and leaving the rest, as teachers have ever done.

3. We can speak out as loudly as we can in order to reclaim our profession. We have chosen this option, adding our voices to those of the students

in this book in the hope that we can amplify theirs. We can speak the common sense of our common belief as educators: That the student is at the center of what we do, not the regulations, not the standards, not the academic disciplines. These are all necessary to what we do, but they are not our priority. Our students are. The students are the subjects we teach to and learn from. Everything else—curriculum, assessments, budgets, buildings—are the objects we use to accomplish that calling.

Student voice is the instrument of change. We are at a point when we and our students must stand up and be heard or the educational policy mongers will continue to strip us of the basic purpose of education, which is to allow our students to dream, reach, and succeed. Our many personal and varied experiences as classroom teachers, along with the experiences of hundreds of educators, teachers, and administrators around the world, tell us that when we do those things, students achieve on multiple levels—personal, social, and of course, academic.

We are responsible for students in their entirety, not just their minds. We face the whole child every day—in every shape, with varied ability, and from every kind of home-life possible. And that's okay. We didn't become educators to pour content into the heads of the brightest students. We did not become educators so that our students could prove to someone in a student-less meeting that we had all made "adequate" progress this year. We certainly did not become educators to teach as if the only thing that mattered was a single test given on a single day. We became educators to make a difference in the lives of our students.

## Three Lessons About Co-Leading

I have found that these are equally true of adults and students.

*Lesson 1—Passion*

During my career, I was incredibly fortunate to have worked alongside some of the finest educators and some of the most involved students in the world. One commonality among many of these individuals strikes me: The adults are extremely passionate and committed to working with students and the students are passionate and committed to working with adults! There is no doubt that experience can make us wiser, but I have also come to realize that passion and commitment are more powerful. You can learn a lot through experience, by listening, researching, observing, and doing. However, it is those with fire in their bellies as well as thoughts in their heads, those with the hunger to make a difference and the belief that they will make the world better who have the power to make a difference in education today. What do both students and adults at your school share a passion about? Work on those things together.

*Lesson 2—Fashion*

The tidal change in politics and its impact on education is staggering. I have seen programs (and people!) at the state and national level getting tossed aside based on political affiliation rather than merit. When will politicians realize that students' learning needs are the same, regardless of whether there is a liberal or a conservative in control? When will students no longer be used as pawns in political posturing, but become meaningful participants in education? When will educational policymakers stop basing decisions on fickle political fashions and start basing them on students' needs? Of course, these are rhetorical questions because the lesson I have learned is: They will not. Therefore, as educators, we need to rise above the political mumbo jumbo and stay true to ourselves and what we believe is best for students, regardless of political affiliation.

*Lesson 3—Action*

If only during my career I had a dollar for every time a promise was expressed, but not delivered, I would be writing books from my bungalow in Bora-Bora. I think we have a tendency in education to say too much and deliver too little. We begin to believe our own rhetoric, even in the absence of concrete actions. We talk of educational reform and new ideas *ad infinitum* . . . and perhaps we think the educational fairies will just make it so. Students sometimes tell us all the great things they are going to do and never lift a finger to make it happen. While I acknowledge that I am becoming more cynical as I get older, it appears to be with good reason! Now, rather than simply accept a person's initial word regarding what he or she believes in and is committed to, I look to see what his or her *actions* say. I hold students and adults to the same standard: What are you *doing* to make a difference?

—RJQ

We know all too well we are being inundated with mandates, and we know we must follow some of those directives. Some requirements have tried to bring equity into our systems and have intentions that are well-meaning. But we must not let common sense be trumped by common practice. What we are trying to say, what we believe the students we have listened to are trying to convey, is that as we perform our duties, we cannot lose touch with the heart of our profession as educators:

- To create Belonging for all students to feel they are valued members of the school, while still maintaining their uniqueness and personal identity.

- To be a Hero to our students to ensure they have someone in their lives who provides unwavering support and guidance.

- To ensure all students have a Sense of Accomplishment and are recognized for the many types of achievement they are capable of, including effort, perseverance, and citizenship.

- To make certain students have Fun & Excitement in our classroom and are engaged and interested in their learning.

- To encourage our students to be Curious & Creative—in order to ask "Why?" and "Why not?" about the world around them.

- To make certain our students have a Spirit of Adventure and feel confident in their ability to take on new and healthy challenges.

- To provide all students Leadership & Responsibility opportunities, thus allowing them to make decisions and accept responsibility for their choices.

- To guarantee that all students leave our classroom with the Confidence to Take Action and the ability to dream about their future, inspired in the present to reach those dreams.

When those basic 8 Conditions are in place, students reach their fullest potential academically, socially, and personally. In a word, they have ASPIRATIONS! This is no less than what was in our hearts when we entered the teaching profession: A hope for the future and the passion and work ethic to succeed.

Traveling the world, reviewing the data we collect, talking to students in focus groups and interviews, hearing from teachers and administrators what is working and what is not, we get frustrated from time to time. Despite decades of educational reform, we are still losing far too many kids—to apathy, to irrelevance, to their game boxes, to say nothing of to the streets. Whether pulled out by the lure of something, anything that seems better than what is happening in school or pushed out by a system that does not value them, involve them, or help them find a direction for their lives, they are lost all the same. They are the worse off for our failing them, and so is our society.

Despite the challenges posed in the current climate, neither of us has ever forgotten why we became educators. Indeed, it has been the very driving force of the research, analysis, and writing that has gone into this text. As the road you travel seems at times a bit rough in your school, never forget what brought you to education in the first place and what keeps you traveling down that road every year, every semester, every day. Never forget that there is no greater profession in this world. Other people make money, and some may even make a living, but those who teach make a difference. The road less traveled in education is the road on which students and teachers are learners *together*, where there is a partnership, where adults do things *with* students, not at, to, or for them. While it's probably not a good idea to take liberties with Robert Frost's iconic poem, we have not come this far without a certain boldness.

Two roads diverged in a wood, and *we,*

*We* took the one less traveled by,

And that has made all the difference

The "we" in this case are adults and students, you and your students. As in the poem, though we have marked the previous, more traveled way of adults as the providers of information, we doubt if we shall ever go back. The road you (plural) travel together in this venture is leading the way for others to follow. You are walking into uncharted territories with your students so that ultimately they can take up the role of guide from you—for themselves, their families, their employers and employees, and for unknown others. Their voice is the instrument of change; your role is to amplify—their voices, their efforts, and their aspirations.

We believe with every ounce of our being that you have the power to make this world better one child, one class, one school, one district at a time. We ask one big favor from you: Never forget that wonderful surprises are just waiting to happen, and all your hopes and dreams for the students you serve are well within your reach.

# References

Amabile, T. M. (1985). Motivation and creativity: Effects of motivational orientation on creative writers. *Journal of Personality and Social Psychology, 48*(2), 393–399.

Anderman, L. H. (2003). Academic and social perceptions as predictors of change in middle school students' sense of belonging. *The Journal of Experimental Education, 72,* 5–22.

Arnone, M. P. (2003). *Using instructional design strategies to foster curiosity.* ERIC Clearinghouse on Information & Technology. Retrieved from http://www.ericdigests .org/2004–3/foster.html.

Black, P., Harrison, C., Lee, C., Marshall, B., & William, D. (2003). *Assessment for learning: Putting it into practice.* Berkshire, England: Open University Press.

Bronson, P., & Merryman, A. (2010, July 10). The creativity crisis. *Newsweek.* Retrieved from http://hartfordinnovationcenter.com/~ARTICLES/O-The%20Creativity%20Crisis-07–19–2010.pdf.

Clarke, M., Haney W., & Madaus, G. (2000). *High stakes testing and high school completion* (Statements, vol. 1, issue 3). Chestnut Hill, MA: National Board on Educational Testing and Public Policy. Carolyn A. and Peter S. Lynch School of Education, Boston College.

Corso, M., Lucey, L., & Fox, K. (2012). Living the mission. *American School Board Journal, 199*(10), 22–24.

Covington, M. V. (2000). Goal theory, motivation, and school achievement: An integrative review. *Annual Review of Psychology, 51*(1), 171–200.

Craft, A. (2005). *Creativity in schools: Tensions and dilemmas.* New York, NY: Routledge.

Csikszentmihalyi, M. (1990). *Flow: The psychology of optimal experience.* New York, NY: Harper & Row.

Damon, W. (2008). *The path to purpose: Helping our children find their calling in life.* New York, NY: Simon & Schuster.

Deci, E., Koestner R., & Ryan R. (2001, Spring). Extrinsic rewards and intrinsic motivation education: Reconsidered once again. *Review of Educational Research, 71*(1), 1–27.

Deci, E. L., & Ryan, R. M. (1985). *Intrinsic motivation and self-determination in human behavior.* New York, NY: Plenum.

Dewey, J. (1938). *Education and experience* (1st Touchstone ed.). New York, NY: Touchstone.

Dweck, C. S. (1986). Motivational processes affecting learning. *American Psychologist, 41*(10), 1040–1048.

Dweck, C. S. (2006). *Mindset: The new psychology of success.* New York, NY: Random House.

Eccles, J., & Wigfield, A. (2002). Motivational beliefs, values, and goals. *Annual Review of Psychology,* 109–133.

Eisner, E. (1994). *The educational imagination: On the design and evaluation of school programs* (3rd ed.). New York, NY: Macmillan College.

Erikson, E. H. (1963). *Childhood and society* (2nd ed.). New York, NY: Norton.

Fielding, M., & Rudduck, J. (2002, September 12–14). *The transformative potential of student voice: Confronting the power issues.* Paper presented at the annual conference of the British Educational Research Association. Retrieved from http://www.leeds.ac.uk/educol/documents/00002544.htm.

Fiestritzer, C. E. (2011). *Profiles of teachers in the U.S. 2011.* Washington, DC: National Center for Education Information. Retrieved from http://www.edweek.org/media/pot2011final-blog.pdf.

Fredricks, J., Blumenfeld, P., & Paris, A. (2004). School engagement: Potential of the concept, state of the evidence. *Review of Educational Research, 74*(1), 59–109.

Fried, R. L. (2001a). *The passionate learner: How teachers and parents can help children reclaim the joy of discovery.* Boston, MA: Beacon Press.

Fried, R. L. (2001b). *The passionate teacher: A practical guide.* Boston, MA: Beacon Press.

Frost, R. (2008). Developing student participation, research and leadership: The HCD student partnership. *School Leadership and Management, 28*(4), 353–368.

Fullan, M. (2007). *The new meaning of educational change.* New York, NY: Teachers College Press.

Furrer, C., & Skinner, E. (2003). Sense of relatedness as a factor in children's academic engagement and performance. *Journal of Educational Psychology, 95*(1), 148–162.

Gallup. (2013, Fall). *U.S. overall Gallup student poll results.* Retrieved from http://www.gallupstudentpoll.com/166037/2013-gallup-student-poll-overall-report.aspx.

Gardner, H. (1983). *Frames of mind.* New York, NY: Basic Books.

Gardner, H. (1993). *The unschooled mind: How children think and how schools should teach.* New York, NY: Basic Books.

Gates, B. (2005, February 26). [Address]. Speech presented at the 2005 National Education Summit on High Schools. [Transcript]. Retrieved from http://www.gatesfoundation.org/media-center/speeches/2005/02/bill-gates-2005-national-education-summit.

Harvard Graduate School of Education. (2011, February). *Pathways to prosperity: Meeting the challenge of preparing young Americans for the 21st century.* Cambridge, MA: Author. Retrieved from http://www.gse.harvard.edu/news_events/features/2011/Pathways_to_Prosperity_Feb2011.pdf.

Henry, K. L., Knight, K. E., & Thornberry, T. P. (2012). School disengagement as a predictor of dropout, delinquency, and problem substance use during adolescence and early adulthood. *Journal of Youth and Adolescence, 41*(2), 156–166.

Jussim, L., & Eccles, J. S. (1992). Teacher expectations II: Construction and reflection of student achievement. *Journal of Personality and Social Psychology, 63*(6), 947–961.

Kim, K. H. (2011). The creativity crisis: The decrease in creative thinking scores on the Torrance Tests of Creative Thinking. *Creativity Research Journal, 23*(4), 285–295.

Klem, A. M., & Connell, J. P. (2005). *Engaging youth in school.* Retrieved from http://www.irre.org/sites/default/files /publication_pdfs/Engaging_Youth_9-8-04.pdf.

Klose, L. M. (2008). Understanding and fostering achievement motivation. *Principal Leadership, 9*(4), 12–16.

Malone, T. W. (1981). Toward a theory of intrinsically motivating instruction. *Cognitive Science, 5*(4), 333–369.

Markus, H., & Nurius, P. (1986). Possible selves. *American Psychologist, 41*(9), 954–969.

Maslow, A. H. (1943). A theory of human motivation. *Psychological Review, 50*(4), 430–437.

Mitra, D. L. (2004). The significance of students: Can increasing student voice in schools lead to gains in youth development? *Teachers College Record, 106,* 651–688.

National Commission on Teaching and America's Future. (2013). *No dream denied: A Pledge to America's Children.* Washington, DC: Author. Retrieved from http://nctaf .org/wp-content/uploads/no-dream-denied_summary_report.pdf.

National Research Council and Institute of Medicine. (2004). *Engaging schools: Fostering high school students' motivation to learn.* Washington, DC: National Academies Press.

Nurmi, J. E. (1991). How do adolescents see their future? A review of the development of future orientation and planning. *Developmental Review, 11*(1), 1–59.

Osterman, K. (2000). Students' need for belonging in the school community. *Review of Educational Research,* 323–367.

Przybylski, A. K., Rigby, C. S., & Ryan, R. M. (2010, June). A motivational model of video game engagement. *Review of General Psychology, 14*(2), 154–166.

Quaglia, R., & Cobb, C. (1996). Toward a theory of student aspirations. *Journal of Research in Rural Education, 12*(3), 127–132.

Quaglia Institute for Student Aspirations. (2013). *My voice national student report (grades 6–12) 2013.* Portland, ME: Author. Retrieved from http://www.qisa.org/.

Reeve, J. (2002). Self-determination theory applied to educational settings. In E. L. Deci & R. M. Ryan (Eds.), *Handbook of self-determination research.* (pp. 183–203). Rochester, NY: University of Rochester Press.

Reeve, J. (2006). Teachers as facilitators: What autonomy-supportive teachers do and why their students benefit. *The Elementary School Journal, 106*(3), 225–236.

Resnick, L. B. (1995). From aptitude to effort: A new foundation for our schools. *Daedalus, 124*(4), 55–62.

Ritchie, C., Flouri, E., & Buchanan, A. (2005). Aspirations and expectations. *Policy Discussion Paper: National Family and Parenting Institute.*

Sagor, R. (2002). Lessons from skateboarders. *Educational Leadership, 60*(1), 34–38.

Schmitt, F. F., & Lahroodi, R. (2008). The epistemic value of curiosity. *Educational Theory, 58*(2), 125–148.

Sherwood Jr., R. (1989). A conceptual framework for the study of aspirations. *Research in Rural Education, 6*(2), 61–66.

Smyth, J. (2006). "When students have power": Student engagement, student voice, and the possibilities for school reform around "dropping out" of school. *International Journal of Leadership in Education, 9*(4), 285–298.

Sterns, E., & Glennie, E. J. (2006). When and why dropouts leave high school. *Youth Society, 38*(1), 29–57.

Tough, P. (2012). *How children succeed: Grit, curiosity, and the hidden power of character.* New York, NY: Houghton Mifflin.

U.S. Department of Education. (2009a). *National Center for Education Statistics, High School Transcript Study.* Retrieved from http://nces.ed.gov/nationsreportcard/pdf/ studies/2011462.pdf.

U.S. Department of Education. (2009b). *National Center for Education Statistics, 2007–08 National Postsecondary Student Aid Study.* Retrieved from http://nces.ed.gov/pubs 2009/2009166.pdf.

Vallerand, R. J., Fortier, M. S., & Guay, F. (1997). Self-determination and persistence in a real-life setting: Toward a motivational model of high school dropout. *Journal of Personality and Social Psychology, 72*(5), 1161–1176.

von Mizener, B. H., & Williams, R. L. (2009). The effects of student choice on academic performance. *Journal of Positive Behavior Interventions, 11*(2), 110–128.

Yazzie-Mintz, E. (2009). *Charting the path from engagement to achievement: A report on the 2009 High School Survey of Student Engagement.* Bloomington, IN: Indiana University, Center for Evaluation and Education Policy. Retrieved from http://ceep.indiana.edu/hssse/images/HSSSE_2010_Report.pdf.

Yonezawa, S., & Jones, M. (2009). Student voices: Generating reform from the inside out. *Theory Into Practice, 48*(3), 205–212.

Yonezawa, S., Jones, M., & Joselowsky, F. (2009). Developing a multidimensional, critical approach to improving engagement for all students. *Journal for Educational Change, 10*(2), 191–209.

# Appendix A

Between fall 2012 and spring 2013, 56,877 students in Grades 6–12 completed the My Voice survey. Two hundred (200) schools from 9 states representing various sizes and socioeconomic backgrounds were included. Forty-nine percent (49%) of the students surveyed were female and 50% were male. Grades 6–12 were represented as follows:

Grade 6: 16%

Grade 7: 17%

Grade 8: 18%

Grade 9: 14%

Grade 10: 13%

Grade 11: 12%

Grade 12: 10%

The participants identified themselves as being from a range of ethnic backgrounds:

White Alone: 63%

Black/African American Alone: 10%

Hispanic/Latino Alone: 6%

American Indian or Native Alaskan Alone: 3%

Asian Alone: 2%

Native Hawaiian Alone: <1%

Other Pacific Islander Alone: <1%

Other Alone: 3%

Two or More Races: 11%

# Appendix B

The tables represented in this appendix are also available in the Quaglia Institute's *My Voice National Student Report 2013* available at www.qisa.org.

Table of Results for All My Voice Statements: Total Agreement, Agreement by Gender, and Agreement by Grade Level

| BELONGING | TOTAL | MALE | FEMALE | 6 | 7 | 8 | 9 | 10 | 11 | 12 |
|---|---|---|---|---|---|---|---|---|---|---|
| School is a welcoming and friendly place. | 66% | 67% | 65% | 73% | 67% | 63% | 65% | 63% | 65% | 68% |
| I feel accepted for who I am at school. | 72% | 76% | 68% | 77% | 72% | 69% | 70% | 69% | 72% | 74% |
| Teachers make an effort to get to know me. | 57% | 59% | 55% | 70% | 62% | 56% | 51% | 48% | 50% | 54% |
| I have difficulty fitting in at school. | 21% | 20% | 22% | 26% | 23% | 22% | 20% | 18% | 17% | 17% |
| Teachers care about my problems and feelings. | 51% | 49% | 52% | 66% | 56% | 50% | 43% | 42% | 43% | 47% |
| I am proud of my school. | 58% | 58% | 58% | 71% | 63% | 53% | 58% | 53% | 51% | 52% |
| I am a valued member of my school community. | 45% | 47% | 44% | 55% | 49% | 45% | 40% | 39% | 42% | 46% |
| I think bullying is a problem in my school. | 49% | 45% | 52% | 58% | 57% | 54% | 44% | 43% | 39% | 36% |
| HEROES | TOTAL | MALE | FEMALE | 6 | 7 | 8 | 9 | 10 | 11 | 12 |
| Students respect teachers. | 41% | 44% | 39% | 54% | 42% | 37% | 37% | 36% | 40% | 43% |
| My parents care about my education. | 95% | 95% | 95% | 97% | 97% | 96% | 95% | 94% | 94% | 92% |

*(Continued)*

(Continued)

| HEROES | TOTAL | MALE | FEMALE | 6 | 7 | 8 | 9 | 10 | 11 | 12 |
|---|---|---|---|---|---|---|---|---|---|---|
| I have a teacher who is a positive role model for me. | 75% | 72% | 79% | 80% | 74% | 73% | 71% | 72% | 77% | 80% |
| Teachers care about me as an individual. | 55% | 55% | 55% | 64% | 58% | 54% | 49% | 48% | 52% | 56% |
| Teachers care if I am absent from school. | 51% | 51% | 51% | 60% | 55% | 49% | 47% | 47% | 47% | 51% |
| If I have a problem, I have a teacher with whom I can talk. | 56% | 54% | 58% | 63% | 57% | 54% | 49% | 51% | 55% | 61% |
| Teachers respect students. | 62% | 62% | 62% | 75% | 67% | 62% | 59% | 55% | 56% | 58% |
| Students respect each other. | 33% | 37% | 29% | 40% | 32% | 29% | 33% | 31% | 33% | 35% |

| SENSE OF ACCOMPLISHMENT | TOTAL | MALE | FEMALE | 6 | 7 | 8 | 9 | 10 | 11 | 12 |
|---|---|---|---|---|---|---|---|---|---|---|
| I am encouraged to practice good citizenship at school. | 77% | 75% | 79% | 87% | 81% | 77% | 74% | 71% | 72% | 73% |
| Teachers recognize students who are kind and helpful. | 73% | 74% | 73% | 82% | 76% | 72% | 70% | 68% | 70% | 73% |
| I have never been recognized for something positive at school. | 25% | 26% | 24% | 26% | 25% | 24% | 26% | 26% | 24% | 24% |
| I give up when schoolwork is difficult. | 18% | 18% | 19% | 14% | 16% | 17% | 21% | 22% | 22% | 20% |
| Teachers recognize me when I try my best. | 60% | 60% | 60% | 69% | 64% | 60% | 55% | 55% | 56% | 59% |
| Teachers let my parents know what I do well. | 51% | 52% | 50% | 71% | 62% | 54% | 43% | 40% | 36% | 36% |
| I put forth my best effort at school. | 77% | 73% | 82% | 87% | 83% | 78% | 74% | 71% | 70% | 70% |
| Getting good grades is important to me. | 91% | 88% | 94% | 95% | 93% | 92% | 90% | 88% | 87% | 86% |

| FUN & EXCITEMENT | TOTAL | MALE | FEMALE | 6 | 7 | 8 | 9 | 10 | 11 | 12 |
|---|---|---|---|---|---|---|---|---|---|---|
| I enjoy being at school. | 54% | 52% | 56% | 62% | 57% | 53% | 53% | 48% | 49% | 49% |
| Teachers enjoy working with students. | 64% | 64% | 63% | 76% | 68% | 62% | 58% | 57% | 60% | 64% |
| Teachers make school an exciting place to learn. | 42% | 44% | 41% | 60% | 48% | 41% | 36% | 34% | 35% | 36% |
| School is boring. | 44% | 47% | 41% | 32% | 39% | 44% | 47% | 50% | 51% | 50% |
| I enjoy participating in my classes. | 66% | 65% | 66% | 75% | 69% | 64% | 63% | 60% | 61% | 62% |
| Teachers have fun at school. | 47% | 49% | 46% | 58% | 51% | 47% | 44% | 41% | 42% | 45% |
| Learning can be fun. | 73% | 71% | 76% | 77% | 73% | 71% | 71% | 71% | 75% | 77% |

| CURIOSITY & CREATIVITY | TOTAL | MALE | FEMALE | 6 | 7 | 8 | 9 | 10 | 11 | 12 |
|---|---|---|---|---|---|---|---|---|---|---|
| I feel comfortable asking questions in class. | 64% | 68% | 61% | 67% | 64% | 62% | 62% | 62% | 66% | 70% |
| My teachers present lessons in different ways. | 76% | 76% | 75% | 84% | 80% | 76% | 73% | 70% | 70% | 71% |
| At school I am encouraged to be creative. | 67% | 69% | 65% | 78% | 73% | 67% | 63% | 60% | 61% | 62% |
| I enjoy working on projects with other students. | 70% | 71% | 69% | 78% | 76% | 73% | 68% | 65% | 63% | 63% |
| My classes help me understand what is happening in my everyday life. | 44% | 46% | 42% | 73% | 67% | 63% | 65% | 63% | 65% | 68% |
| School inspires me to learn. | 65% | 62% | 67% | 76% | 69% | 65% | 61% | 58% | 57% | 59% |
| I enjoy learning new things. | 80% | 79% | 81% | 83% | 79% | 78% | 78% | 79% | 83% | 85% |
| I learn new things that are interesting to me at school. | 72% | 71% | 73% | 82% | 75% | 71% | 69% | 69% | 68% | 69% |
| What I learn in school will benefit my future. | 79% | 77% | 81% | 88% | 84% | 81% | 77% | 74% | 70% | 71% |

*(Continued)*

(Continued)

| SPIRIT OF ADVENTURE | TOTAL | MALE | FEMALE | 6 | 7 | 8 | 9 | 10 | 11 | 12 |
|---|---|---|---|---|---|---|---|---|---|---|
| I like challenging assignments. | 41% | 40% | 41% | 47% | 40% | 39% | 36% | 37% | 41% | 44% |
| I push myself to do better academically. | 84% | 81% | 88% | 88% | 86% | 85% | 82% | 81% | 81% | 80% |
| Students are supportive of each other. | 41% | 42% | 39% | 48% | 40% | 37% | 40% | 38% | 40% | 42% |
| I am afraid to try something if I think I may fail. | 32% | 28% | 37% | 36% | 35% | 33% | 33% | 32% | 30% | 25% |
| Teachers help me learn from my mistakes. | 65% | 66% | 65% | 79% | 72% | 66% | 61% | 57% | 58% | 59% |
| I want to do my best at school. | 88% | 84% | 92% | 94% | 91% | 89% | 88% | 86% | 84% | 84% |
| I am excited to tell my friends when I get good grades. | 60% | 54% | 66% | 71% | 66% | 61% | 56% | 55% | 54% | 52% |

| LEADERSHIP & RESPONSIBILITY | TOTAL | MALE | FEMALE | 6 | 7 | 8 | 9 | 10 | 11 | 12 |
|---|---|---|---|---|---|---|---|---|---|---|
| Students have a voice in decision making at school. | 46% | 46% | 46% | 61% | 53% | 45% | 44% | 39% | 36% | 37% |
| I see myself as a leader. | 67% | 66% | 67% | 69% | 66% | 66% | 64% | 65% | 66% | 70% |
| Other students see me as a leader. | 37% | 38% | 36% | 37% | 35% | 36% | 35% | 36% | 39% | 43% |
| Teachers encourage students to make decisions. | 72% | 71% | 72% | 78% | 75% | 72% | 69% | 68% | 68% | 70% |
| Teachers are willing to learn from students. | 52% | 52% | 52% | 65% | 57% | 53% | 48% | 44% | 44% | 46% |
| I am a good decision maker. | 68% | 69% | 68% | 69% | 68% | 66% | 67% | 68% | 70% | 73% |
| I know the goals my school is working on this year. | 49% | 49% | 49% | 63% | 56% | 50% | 45% | 41% | 40% | 41% |

| CONFIDENCE TO TAKE ACTION | TOTAL | MALE | FEMALE | 6 | 7 | 8 | 9 | 10 | 11 | 12 |
|---|---|---|---|---|---|---|---|---|---|---|
| I believe I can be successful. | 94% | 93% | 94% | 94% | 94% | 93% | 93% | 93% | 94% | 94% |
| I believe I can make a difference in this world. | 71% | 69% | 72% | 73% | 70% | 69% | 69% | 69% | 71% | 75% |
| Teachers believe in me and expect me to be successful. | 75% | 75% | 76% | 82% | 79% | 76% | 72% | 71% | 71% | 74% |
| Going to college is important to my future. | 87% | 84% | 91% | 91% | 90% | 89% | 86% | 85% | 85% | 85% |
| I work hard to reach my goals. | 85% | 82% | 87% | 90% | 87% | 85% | 82% | 81% | 81% | 83% |
| I am excited about my future. | 85% | 83% | 88% | 88% | 87% | 85% | 84% | 83% | 83% | 85% |
| I think it is important to set high goals. | 85% | 82% | 87% | 88% | 86% | 84% | 83% | 82% | 84% | 85% |
| I know the kind of person I want to become. | 82% | 80% | 84% | 83% | 82% | 82% | 80% | 80% | 82% | 84% |
| School is preparing me well for my future. | 70% | 68% | 72% | 82% | 78% | 73% | 68% | 64% | 60% | 59% |

# Index

**CORWIN**
A SAGE Company

The Corwin logo—a raven striding across an open book—represents the union of courage and learning. Corwin is committed to improving education for all learners by publishing books and other professional development resources for those serving the field of PreK–12 education. By providing practical, hands-on materials, Corwin continues to carry out the promise of its motto: **"Helping Educators Do Their Work Better."**